Moments In Between

The Art of the Quiet Mind

Conari Press

David Kundtz

First published in 2006 by Conari Press,
an imprint of Red Wheel/Weiser, LLC
With offices at:
500 Third Street, Suite 230
San Francisco, CA 94107
www.redwheelweiser.com

Design copyright © 2006 Conari Press
Text copyright © 2000 by David Kundtz
All rights reserved. No part of this
publication may be reproduced or
transmitted in any form or by any means,
electronic or mechanical, including
photocopying, recording, or by any
information storage and retrieval system,
without permission in writing from Red
Wheel/Weiser, LLC. Reviewers may quote
brief passages. Portions of this book were
originally published in 2000 by Conari
Press as *Everyday Serenity* under ISBN:
1-57324-162-8.

ISBN-10: 1-57324-276-4
ISBN-13: 978-1-57324-276-9

Photography credits: *Animal Vegetable
Mineral* Bill Bachman © Digital Vision: 8,
24, 35, 44, 56, 77, 85, 88, 100, 107, 114,
123. *Study of Form and Color* Anthony Ise ©
Photodisc: 1, 6, 20, 28, 30, 42, 49, 53, 60,
64, 68, 72, 80, 82, 92, 96, 104, 108, 118.
Flowers © Corbis: 12, 17, 39, 111, 128.

Book design by Kathleen Wilson Fivel
Typeset in Linotype Avenir and
Monotype Bembo

Printed in China
MD

10 9 8 7 6 5 4 3

I dedicate this book of reflections
to all the clients, past and present,
of my counseling practice
in gratitude for your trust.

Your stories are for me,
without exception, pure grace.

It is because artists do not practice, patrons
do not patronize, crowds do not assemble to
reverently worship the great work of Doing
Nothing, that the world has lost its philosophy....

—G. K. Chesterton

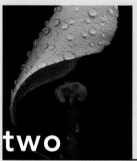

A New Way of Dealing with Life

Welcome

Welcome to a new way to cope with the demands of a too-busy life.

Welcome to a way that requires no difficult skills, adds no new burdens, and accommodates all spiritual systems and life-styles.

Welcome to all who want to do nothing—more often, more creatively, with joy, and without guilt.

Welcome to one-minute retreats that can be yours at any time of the day or night.

Welcome to a quiet mind—tranquility, calmness, and clarity—in the midst of a too-busy world.

Welcome to moments of both rest and insight.

Welcome to a quiet mind and the moments in between.

David Kundtz
Kensington, California

one
Still Moments in Busy Days

Sounding Well

Rests, as I understand them, are those moments in a piece of music when there is a passage of time but no sound. There is nothing. So Schoenberg, the composer, says that "nothing" always sounds well.

Hmm. Sounds like a trick, or a riddle. What's wrong with this statement? Buddhists might call Schoenberg's words a koan, a paradoxical riddle with no answer, used for discussion and teaching.

What can we make of it?

What gives life to the music is the feeling that jumps in during those pauses, during those sometimes incredibly quick split seconds when one note is just finishing its last echoing vibrations, but before the next one takes up the progression. The feeling slips, quick as a wink, into the gap and brings soul and life to the music. It is first felt, then expressed, by the composer. Then it is reborn with a familiarity, but also with the somehow new and unique contribution of each performer.

The feeling lives in the rests. And not just with the rests in music, but with the rests in bus driving and kindergarten teaching and homemaking and managing and selling advertising and cooking supper and picking up the kids and phoning customers and writing reports and on and on. The feeling lives in what you put into the rests. And the rests always sound well!

The quiet moments—rests—in your day make your whole day sound well.

> *Rests always sound well.*
> —**Arnold Schoenberg**

> As you go about your day today, notice the rests in the rhythm of the day.

Rat Race

The metaphor of the rat race as a way to talk about the nature of contemporary life is instructive. I wonder about its origin. And just what is a rat race? I picture a maze in some scientific laboratory with a dozen rodents scrambling in all directions, trying with great frustration to find their way to freedom. Is that a rat race? Did anyone tell the rats they were in a race? Is there really a winner in a rat race?

And that we should choose this metaphor as a way to talk about the way we live our lives is . . . what? Alarming? "Well, we've got to get going and join the rat race." We do?

The metaphors we use not only reflect the way we live, but create the way we live. If we call life a rat race, it will tend to become one.

So let's change metaphors. Here are a few suggestions:

Life is a cat prowl. I envision slow and careful steps, a calm awareness of what is going on in my neighborhood, and a pace that suits my needs.

Life is a dog walk. I move now with lively interest, with stoppings and goings, encounters with other dogs, trees, and people, always ready to respond to a friendly petting.

Life is a fox trot. Here is a bouncy-stepped way to dance through life. Find a partner! You can always sit the next one out.

Life is a monkey march. Life is a pony canter. Life is a whale breach. Life is a swallow soar. Life is a pig parade. Life is an elephant lope. Life is a bear excursion (the one I'd pick).

The trouble with the rat race is even if you win, you're still a rat.

—Lily Tomlin

Spend a quiet time today and pick your metaphor for life's journey.

Every Day

These are the things Goethe wanted in his day, every day. What do you want in yours?

Here is a snippet from a conversation I overheard in a busy downtown store between two middle-aged women:

"It's so good to see you. We just don't seem to get together as much any more, and it seems so many of us are saying the same thing. Why is that?" said one.

"I know exactly what you mean," said the other. "It seems that there's always just too much going on."

I'm convinced we all really do know what is happening to the way we are in the world, compared to the way we want to be. As the woman said, there's always just too much going on. The problem is not what we don't know; it's that we somehow feel powerless to change it.

When you have begun dealing with the problem of too much going on, you can start to identify just what you want to include in your "every day."

Even when you get together with your friend, you might discover that Goethe wasn't far off the mark. With your friend you might hear a little song (listen to some favorite music), read a good poem (discuss an article you recently read), see a fine picture (visit a museum or show a photo of your grandkids), or speak a few reasonable words (have an enjoyable conversation, catching up on each other's lives).

One ought, every day at least, to hear a little song, read a good poem, see a fine picture, and, if it were possible, to speak a few reasonable words.

—**Goethe**

> Today take some moments to decide what you want your "every day" to include. Repeat every day forever.

Going to the Post Office

You may depend on it," Thoreau continues, "that poor fellow who walks away with the greatest number of letters, proud of his extensive correspondence, has not heard from himself this long while."

I think I know the cause of our cultural, spiritual, and social problems today, just as Thoreau knew 150 years ago. Our inward life is failing.

Many of us know this, of course, and just knowing it doesn't change things. But what if someone—maybe you—could convince ten or twenty people to stop going to the post office for their information, and instead to stay quiet and recollected for a few minutes or even an hour a day to attend to their "inward lives"? What if I could do the same?

I used to think that what we needed was a saint or a prophet: a modern-day Francis of Assisi who would call us to our senses by the power of his example and love; or a Joan of Arc to inspire us with her disdain for the acceptable, her single-mindedness, and her devotion to her voices.

But we have saints; we've always had saints, canonized or not. We've always had prophets who are well attuned to their inward lives, who have voices of passion and love, voices of virtue and wisdom, who live lives of example and service, and who call us to the same.

And still many of us keep on stumbling to the post office.

In proportion as our inward life fails, we go constantly and desperately to the post office.

—Henry David Thoreau

Today, find a way to redirect your trip to the post office to a journey to your inward life.

Permission to Stop

The author's words are a complaint that he had to have justification for doing nothing. He and his friends could not do nothing just because they wanted to; they had to have a very good reason, such as divorce. Then they could justify taking time off, or "wasting valuable time"—they had an excuse. They had just gone through something painful, and people would be hesitant to criticize them. Their guilt would be minimal.

But then he wisely throws out that kind of thinking and gives himself permission—no justification necessary—for doing nothing.

Unnecessary self-restrictions and false guilt burden many of us and keep us from the peaceful times we yearn for. Quiet time to be alone is not an optional nicety; nor is it just for the retired, the lazy, or those naturally inclined. It is for all of us. It is valuable time well spent.

And above all, it needs no justification other than its own noble purpose: to become more fully awake and to remember what you most need to remember about yourself and your life.

The only way we could justify sitting motionless in an A-frame cabin in the north woods...was if we had just survived a really messy divorce.

—Ian Frazier

Do you need permission for doing nothing? Here it is! Use it today.

Finally Getting It

O ften I find it difficult to get across the idea of doing nothing. I first discovered the resistance to the idea in myself. I continue to discover it in other people.

We are just not used to doing nothing. It sounds and feels and seems wrong somehow. We want to fill up the time with something.

At a recent mini-seminar at a bookstore, a young man, about seventeen, entered late, wearing his hat backward and carrying a skateboard. He sat down in the middle of the front row and paid close attention to what I was saying.

Midway through the presentation he raised his hand and said, "What you're saying is that we should spend a lot of time just thinking about the really important things in life, right?"

"Nooo," I answered, "I'm suggesting that's something we should *not* do! Just do nothing, don't try to think about anything!" My answer was met with a vexed and quizzical look. The look remained, and as I continued the seminar his attention stayed focused on my answer to his question, and not on what I was saying.

After a little while, he stood up quite suddenly, smiled at me, gathered up his skateboard and backpack, and began to leave.

"So long," I said, interrupting my presentation. All eyes were on him as he took the opportunity to say, "So long! Oh, and thanks for Nothing. I appreciate it!"

I think he meant it.

Thanks for Nothing!

—A young seminar participant

Today, consider the question: What is my understanding of doing nothing?

Reality Check

O ccasionally someone will say to me, "Just sitting and doing nothing seems to be running from the real world, hiding from what you don't want to face." My response is to reiterate that intentionally doing nothing is indeed the *opposite* of running and hiding. This is *because* it brings you face-to-face with—even to the point of embracing—the most important and challenging aspects of human life, those based on your meanings and values.

As Eliot says, if you want roses, plant trees. What doing nothing can do is help you *know* what you really want—is it roses, or gladiolas, or redwoods, or none of those?—so that you don't end up with a beautiful garden of what you don't want.

The English novelist quoted above, George Eliot, speaks these words from personal experience. Born Mary Anne Evans into the male-dominated Victorian world, she led her rich and complex life successfully competing in the theological and literary worlds of her time. Her masculine pen name increased the power she needed in order to be all she wanted to be, not running and hiding, just embracing life as she saw it, and in the era in which she saw it.

No waiting for a rain of roses for her.

It will never rain roses: When we want to have more roses we must plant more trees.

—George Eliot

Today consider if you are waiting for a rain of roses.

New Eyes

A significant challenge to any seminar presenter is the problem of follow-up or continuity: What is going to allow the participants to keep their new insights fresh and accessible? What would keep the information from fading into the fog of forgetting, which the passage of time seems to engender? It's typical for participants to leave the seminar with the best of intentions and enthusiasm, and just as typical for participants to lose them in a few weeks.

One response to this challenge is to base the seminar on the skill of having new eyes. If you leave with new eyes, the follow-up problem takes care of itself; everything you see from now on will be a new discovery.

You will have a new and different way of seeing something that you have been looking at all your life.

Something such as "doing nothing": Today I am going to use new eyes with which to see "doing nothing."

For today, please see time spent doing nothing not with your old eyes, not as a waste of time, not as boring, not as unproductive, not as guilt-ridden laziness. Now, please see it with new eyes, as very fertile time, as urgently necessary and life-giving time, in which to wake up and remember who you are.

See it as the most important time of your life.

The problem of follow-up disappears when you have new eyes.

The real voyage of discovery consists not in seeking new landscapes, but in having new eyes.

—Marcel Proust

Today bring new eyes, rather than new landscapes, to what you want to discover.

Road Rage

I wonder if you have the same experience that I sometimes do. I'm driving along, thinking that I am in a fine mood, when the driver waiting at a stoplight in front of me puts on his left turn signal just as the light turns green. The reaction is immediate and strong: I am absolutely furious! I struggle not to lay on the horn and do a few other things as well.

How can I go from serenity to rage in an instant? And because of such a thing as a left turn? Can't I really afford the thirty seconds or minute that I'll have to wait? What happened? What's going on in me?

The only answer I can come up with is that the car has become a symbol of so many of the societal frustrations we experience today. The classic symbol of our independence now often thwarts our progress and becomes an inconvenience and a limit on our freedom, not a means to it.

For a serene life, we need to pay a lot of attention to driving automobiles, whether or not we actually drive.

I propose spending some time getting to know your car—well, not your car, really, but getting to know yourself in your car. Think about how you want to react to other drivers, talk to family members and friends about your common experiences while driving, and perhaps change your expectations of what driving will actually be like for you—more traffic, more delays, more jams.

And if the rage hits you anyway, remember to take a deep breath or two—always do that. Then see what you can come up with to restore serenity. I try to think of the fact that I'm only one of many trying to get somewhere. And if I'm feeling particularly honest, I recall that sometimes I am the one putting on the left turn signal just as the light turns green.

There is no class of person more moved by hate than the motorist.

—C. R. Hewitt

Spend some time with your car today.

two

Making Room for Life

Something from Nothing

When our creative thinking has come to a halt and our thoughts are caught in fruitless repetitive circles, it is time to stop and allow our minds to meander.

This was certainly true for Elias Howe, who lived in the mid-1800s and is credited with inventing the sewing machine. The story goes that one day, as he was working on the sewing machine project, he became particularly frustrated. He had been working with a regular sewing needle and had tried many different ways to mechanize it, with no success.

He decided to take a break from his efforts and sat at the window of his workshop, gazing out in reverie. He later told his wife what happened:

> As I wandered in my mind, a remarkable scene came to me. I was in a deep jungle and I was in a big, black pot with a roaring fire under it. I was being cooked alive! A warrior came at me with spear raised and ready to thrust.
>
> But what I noticed at that moment was something very curious about the spear: It had a hole in its tip.

The pivotal discovery in the invention of the sewing machine is that the hole for the thread goes in the tip of the needle, not at its other end, as in a regular needle. The breakthrough had eluded the inventor in his conscious intellectual efforts, but came to him poetically, graphically, in his moment of reverie.

Creativity thrives on doing nothing. In the moments that might seem empty, what has been there all along in some embryonic form is given space and comes to life.

One of the greatest necessities in America is to discover creative solitude.

—Carl Sandburg

Today, bring the gift of doing nothing to your challenges that need creative solutions.

What We Often Miss

As you might guess, I love epigraphs, those pithy sayings that capture an important idea in a few, happy words. Each of these reflections begins with an epigraph. There are many that I like, but if I had to choose my favorite, on many days I would choose the one above.

Consider the magnificence of the moments when we remember the Ojibwa saying. Any of the moments of your life can become a wonder, any situation you're in can be affected by transcendent joy.

The two of us are in the grocery store, doing the shopping for the week. We are a bit annoyed with each other. You pick out some things, I others. There are a few questions—"Do we have enough milk? How many bagels should we get?"—but mostly we are both focused on what we are doing; our care for each other is not expressed in clear ways. Actually, I am feeling sorry for myself, having to put up with your moods. (But remember, a great wind is bearing us right now dramatically, miraculously across the sky!)

Some friends have stopped by at a very inconvenient time. I have planned a couple of projects that I've wanted to do for a long time. I am trying to be nice, trying to be patient. I wish they would go. I wish they never came. (But remember, a magnificent wind is enfolding us all in its arms and bearing us—imagine!—across the sky!)

Especially when you're feeling sorry for yourself, let your pity be a trigger for a Stillpoint that will transport you across the sky.

Sometimes I go about in pity for myself, and all the while a great wind is bearing me across the sky.

—Ojibwa saying

Today, be awake to the Great Wind in the midst of stress or routine.

Doing and Being

middle-aged married couple find themselves trying to deal with a less than perfect marriage. In their discussion the wife asks her husband, a physician, why he spends so much time at work. "What is it you get at work that you don't get at home?"

Her husband answers, "When I'm at work it's the only time I feel like I know who I really am."

Being a doctor has become who he is, not just what he does. When he is at home there is no need for a doctor, but much need for a husband, father, homemaker, family man, caregiver, short-order cook, Mr. Fix-it, neighbor, playmate, friend, and so on. But he is a doctor and thus cannot respond with any enthusiasm or authenticity to all his other roles.

If he could learn to see that doctoring is something he does, that it is his work, as well as possibly a source of much of joy and fulfillment, then he could be free to do lots of other things as well, and just be himself. As it is, when he returns home he is still a doctor. Most of the time nobody there needs a doctor. So he floats around unengaged, bored, and causing trouble.

Doing nothing can help you if you find yourself in the doctor's situation. Be still and be with yourself. By *doing nothing* the *doing* part of you drops away and the *being* part of you gradually comes alive. It has to, because the doing is gone.

The irony is that the more you separate what you are from what you do, the more you can do!

If you are what you do, when you don't you aren't.

—Quoted by William Byron, S.J.

Consider: If you were no longer to do what you do, who would you be?

23

Getting to the True Self

My client was worried. Her mother, a widow of about sixty, had become ill quite suddenly. My client was the only available relative and thus responsible for her mother's care.

When she came in for her weekly session, my client's main concern was about the surgeon who was to operate on her mother. When she tried to make an appointment with this doctor to learn about the procedure, this is what she experienced: It was difficult to get to the doctor; he had gatekeepers with endless excuses. But he also had a reputation of being a good surgeon.

When she did finally get a moment of his time, she experienced him as impatient, stressed, self-impressed, and not at all relaxed. His smile was forced, too quick, and seemed insincere. He didn't look her in the eye while speaking to her, and he had to check his notes for her mother's name and condition.

My client went home and spent about an hour in quiet reflection. Then she called the surgeon and declined his service.

"I can't believe I did that!" was her comment, "but he just didn't seem present to the moment at all. I felt he was always putting his attention somewhere else, not on me, nor on my mother. I just didn't sense he cared."

The doctor's too-stressed life—and whatever else—did not allow him a tranquil and wholly relaxed mind and thus he did not access what Indira Gandhi calls his own "true image." My client wanted someone who was wholly present to himself to operate on her mother. So would I.

The mind can only reflect the true image of the Self when it is tranquil and wholly relaxed.

—Indira Gandhi

No matter how busy you are, spend relaxing time today to give life to your true self.

25

Just Sit

People who are at ease with themselves are a wonderful gift to the world. They model for us with a power that words can never match.

When I was a boy, I had Satchel Paige's picture on my wall, along with about fifteen other Cleveland Indian baseball players. Satchel had a special attraction. He not only became the first African American pitcher in the American League (at the age of forty-two), he was also full of joy, wisdom, and showmanship. He just loved life, even though, especially at its beginning, it didn't offer him much.

He could pitch words as well as he could pitch a baseball. The above words are an example. Satchel always had his eye on the crowd and knew how to give them what they wanted, and sometimes what they needed as well.

In my memory of him, I realize that he always had quietness, serenity, and even a sense of slowness about him—even though he was famous for his fastball—almost as if he were always remembering something important, something he didn't want to forget. His smile took a while to complete itself, and he had an easy grace in his movements.

Is there someone in your life who is a model of serenity for you? What gives them such a calm in the storm of life? How can you cultivate that in yourself?

Sometimes I sits and thinks, and sometimes I just sits.

—Satchel Paige

Today, find yourself a model of serenity and make yourself an apprentice.

Oops!

It seems to be characteristic of the young to rush so fast through life that they miss the best parts. But I seem to have been fairly adept at dragging that youthful characteristic along with me well into my adult years. I still have to remind myself not to hurry past my pleasure. (I often need to give this advice to myself when I am eating: My tendency is to eat too fast and not savor the food, and thus miss the pleasure.)

Businesspeople seem particularly prone to this tendency from my observation. It must be the nature of doing business, competitive and fast, and the fact that the winner—the best in the business—gets the prize of financial success.

Many successful climbers of the corporate ladder later recognize themselves as those who were so intent, so earnest, so hardworking, moving with such breathless haste up the ladder, that they happened to miss a vital element in their pursuit: the ladder was leaning against the wrong wall.

When they arrive at the top, it hits them. For example, "Oops! I am a top executive, but what I really wanted was to be a writer." Looking back, they can recognize what they had hurried past: the high school teacher who encouraged them to write, the college prize won for essay writing, the longing to create a novel—all missed, hurried past.

Noticing and recognizing pleasures is what we gain from our moments of doing nothing, of reverie, of awakening to our true desires and passions.

It is never too late to find a new wall or climb a different ladder.

Most men pursue pleasure with such breathless haste they hurry past it.

—Sören Kierkegaard

Do you have an "Oops" to say about what you've hurried past?

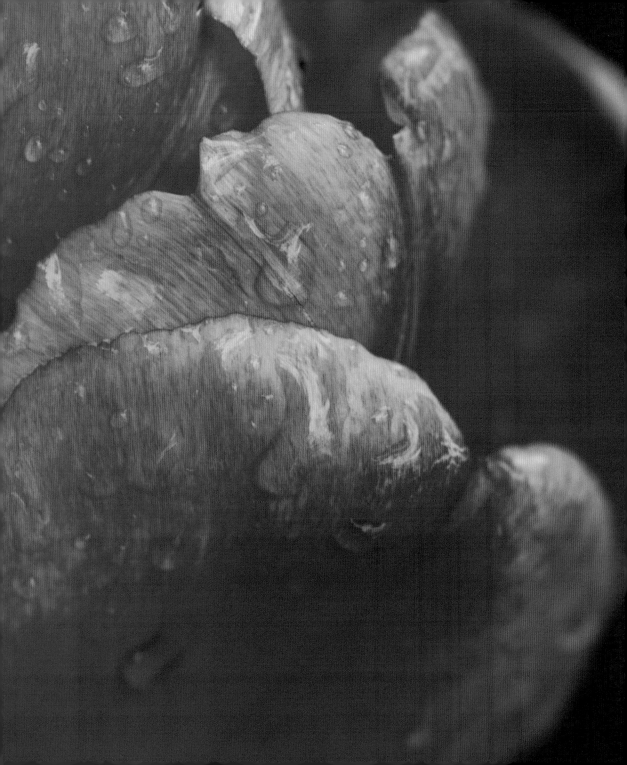

Thoughts Unsought

Where do they come from, these unsought thoughts? Pope John XXIII tells the way he first thought about convening the Second Vatican Council, which has been called the most significant religious event of the century and will influence the world for centuries to come.

He said, although not with Locke's words, that the idea for the Council just dropped into his mind. It did not come as a logical answer to a particular problem. It just dropped in, so to speak. Lawrence Elliott, in his biography of the popular pope, quotes him: "Suddenly an inspiration sprang up within us as a flower that blooms in an unexpected springtime... a council!"

I won't attempt to answer the question about where these ideas come from. But let me say something about not missing them when they do come. And not just to popes.

We won't miss these gems only if we have prepared ourselves in advance of their visit by creating a place of welcome, if we have a sign on our souls saying: Valuable Unsought Thoughts—Enter Here.

The construction of the sign includes the wood of silence, the metal of serenity, and the nails of quiet recollection.

Pope John is a fine example of such a soul. His autobiography reveals a lifelong desire and effort to "know and do God's will." When the thought of the Council dropped in, his place of welcome was ready, having been prepared by prayer, service, humility, and many hours and days of contemplation.

> *The thoughts that often come unsought, and, as it were, drop into the mind, are commonly the most valuable of any we have.*
>
> **—John Locke**

See your quiet moments today as preparation of a welcoming place for valuable thoughts that will just drop in.

three
Remembering to Take the Time

A Lesson from Sister

I can still hear my seventh grade teacher's voice: "David, go to your place! Be still and pay attention!" She didn't say "Be quiet!" but always "Be still!", which implies not only a lack of noise but a lack of movement as well, a quietude of the whole person.

You have long since left the realm of schoolchildren, but these words are just as important—no, more important—because now you can know their real power: Practicing stillness and attention can change your life, especially as your practice gains power and effectiveness.

Here are a few questions to consider:

What is your way of being still? In which place are you likely to be when you are still—inside, outside, in a particular room or space? In what posture would you tend to be—sitting, standing, lying down?

Are you someone for whom being still is particularly difficult or challenging? Could you practice being still while walking?

When you are indeed still, to what is your attention drawn? How do you think about paying attention? That is, what does it mean to you?

Armed with this description of what paying attention looks like for you, you won't miss the opportunities to practice it. You will be ready when the moments for stillness come.

Sit down, be still, and pay attention!

—Sister Mary Odilo

Today pick a few moments to sit down, be still, and pay attention.

Telephones, Beepers, and Clocks

The most frequent challenge I hear from busy people who want to find peace in their daily lives is that they have goodwill, but they just plain forget to take a few moments for a Stillpoint. At the end of the day they realize they only did one or two, or even none.

What helps me, and many of the people I speak with, is finding triggers. Look for the triggers in your day—moments, people, situations, times, places, events, goings, comings—that have these traits in common: (1) They are frequent. (2) They are automatic. (3) They are consistent.

Here is an example: telephones, beepers, and clocks, or—putting a spin on John Donne's words—bells that sound in your environment. When you hear them, you can Stop, take a breath, and remember who you are—every time you hear the phone, the clock, the doorbell, or a beeper.

Here's one I do. Every time I hear the microwave beeper—a sound I find annoying—I call myself to a momentary breath of relaxation and a recollection of how I'll enjoy whatever is being warmed.

Here are a few helps to establish an event or a sound as a trigger. Place sticky notes or other signs on things; put things "out of place" to remind you; take a few moments at the beginning of the day and put your Stillpoints in your imagination: *When I take a bathroom break, I will stay there for one minute longer, close my eyes and notice what I am feeling physically in my body or emotionally.*

It takes a while to establish the practice, so don't get discouraged. Stick with it. If you do, I'll guarantee you will become good at it and, more important, the quality of your day will leap forward.

Never send to know for whom the bell tolls; it tolls for thee.

—John Donne

Right now, think of two triggers in your day—bells that toll for thee.

32

Breathe!

It is impossible to overemphasize the importance of deep, conscious breathing. Its benefits are numerous and profound, far beyond what one might expect from an activity so common and automatic.

The tendency in our speeded-up world is to breathe shallow, quick breaths that contribute to our general feeling of tightness and hurry.

As you breathe in, close your eyes and allow the breath to gently push your stomach out, pause there for a brief moment, then breathe out as your stomach returns to normal. As you breathe out, allow your jaw and shoulders to drop in an easy manner. Relax and feel the relaxation flow from the top of your head down to your fingertips. Stay still for a moment and then repeat the breathing.

Remember to breathe this way as often as you can. Every breath can bring us to a moment of peace and tranquillity.

Remember especially when you are nervous, upset, angry, stressed, on stage, concentrating, rushed, or in so many other tense moments that seem so frequent these days.

As the Vietnamese monk and teacher Thich Nhat Hanh reminds us, when we breathe, there is an automatic connection between soul and body; we are brought to an awareness of our spiritual natures by the physical act of breathing.

Our breath is the bridge from our body to our mind.

—Thich Nhat Hanh

"Things to do today: Exhale, inhale, exhale. Ahhh."
(Jack Kornfield)

Pick a Day for a Stopover

Today I issue you a challenge: It's a very practical way to put into practice Horace's encouragement. Sit down with your calendar and seize the day! Pick out a day within a few months during which you will do a Stopover, that is, a whole day in which you will do nothing. I know it might be scary. You probably think you're too busy. But I am encouraging you to take a risk and try it. I'm fairly sure that the experience will be such that you will want to do it again and again.

Chose a day during which you are sure you will have nothing else you must do. Then mark that day on your calendar with a big *S* for your time of creatively doing nothing.

As the day approaches, you can anticipate it, wondering, for example, "What in the world will I do with all that time with nothing to do?" (Answer: nothing). Resist planning anything except perhaps going to some place that will facilitate your Stopover, like a beach, a park, or a retreat house. Or just plan to stay home. Make a determination to stay with it.

Remember to prepare the other people in your life. Too often, they will not encourage you, finding many reasons why this does not sound like a good idea, or even seems a little weird. You'll probably find that the idea pushes people's limits a bit. Remind them from time to time that your Stopover day is coming. It might be best to refer to it simply as some quiet time. Find ways and places to assure you will not be disturbed.

When the planning is finished you can just look forward with anticipation!

Seize the day!

—Horace

Today: Mark an S (for seize!) on a day in your calendar for a Stopover.

Going Within

A Stillpoint involves ceasing what you are doing, breathing, and turning your focus within yourself. Some of us are quite comfortable going within ourselves, and do it regularly; others are not so comfortable and find the process daunting and unfamiliar. If you are in the latter group please heed the advice above and be patient with yourself. Keep in mind a few ideas:

This need not be complicated. The going in does not have to be an active searching for something, but rather simply an awareness, a quiet looking. It is more passive than active. Just being still.

You probably focus within regularly but just don't call it that. You might find, with naturalist John Muir, that "going out [into Nature]... was really going in."

Remember to breathe.

Here are a few thoughts to help you get started going within:

What feeling do I notice right now? (Try not to answer what you are thinking.)

Can I pick a word or two which would come close to describing the current state of my soul?

Name a few virtues you know are yours (such as kindness, goodwill, empathy ...). Does one describe what you see inside yourself now?

If you aren't used to going within, you will need to be patient with yourself. . . .

—Barbara De Angelis

Throughout the day today, turn your focus in to become more awake.

Remembering Who You Are

The priest or minister in some Christian traditions uses these words as he rubs ashes on your forehead on the first day of Lent, Ash Wednesday. They are meant to help us remember death. It gets right to the point. Ideally, such remembering calls one to a conversion of life, puts things in perspective, so that first things are indeed first, last things last.

But we have more things to remember than the fact that we will die: what we desire, who we love, what we have chosen as goals and ideals, where we've come from, where we're going, who we want with us, the road we're taking, what we need for the journey, our ultimate values, what is most meaningful, and so on.

Remembering is the part of the Stillpoint when you call to mind something meaningful. But the nature of a Stillpoint is to be brief, so the remembering often is a concentrated or abbreviated expression that stands for the reality it symbolizes. Here are some examples:

A word, or a few words: Patience. Relax. Peace. Home. Be here now. *Memento mori.* I am with you. I can do it.

An image of a sacred place, a spiritual leader, a family member, a symbol, an event, a prayer.

A value, an ideal, a virtue in a gesture, such as clasping your hands, extending your arms, bowing your head, raising your eyes, touching index finger with thumb to create a circle.

An intention-for-the-day that you made in the morning.

What are the things you want to remember? By making them a part of your daily Stillpoints, think of all the remembering you can do in a year!

Remember that thou are dust, and unto dust thou shall return.

—from the liturgy of Ash Wednesday

Determine what you want to remember today during your Stillpoints. Pick a symbol to express it.

Opening

When we take daily time to remember who we are and what is important to us, we can be more open to life. If we are not open, we miss so much! Being open means the realities of life have a way to get into you, the gates are open, and you won't miss what you don't want to miss.

One of the ways to open all your pores is to find an image that signifies opening to you. An image is instantaneous, takes little effort, and has a powerful effect on us. (A picture is worth a thousand words.)

Here are a few examples of images of openness that might get you started in finding your own:

A dish antenna: open to all the signals of the universe

A sapling: stretching to reach the sun and rain

A whale: huge maw agape and swimming through the krill

A magnet: attracting your opposites

A child: knowing that everything is possible

When we race through life never stopping, openness is difficult because too much goes right through us, without making any difference in our lives.

In the words quoted above, Thoreau uses the analogy of bathing. Perhaps that could be the image for you: When you are immersed in a tub or standing under a steady shower of water, no part of you is missed. You are open.

Open all your pores and bathe in all the tides of nature.

—Henry David Thoreau

Pick a metaphor for openness (perhaps from the list above). Three times today stop and recall your image.

Filling In

Picture yourself at your moments of transition, especially when they are sudden or quick or involve dramatic change: As you move from the frantic pace of work to the quiet pace of home (or, indeed, its opposite); as you leave a day of solitary work to join a large group of talking people; as you move from the loudness of a fifth-grade classroom to the silence of the walk home; as you move from a bustling city to a country village; as you face a solitary life after a long life of companionship.

Each transition brings with it a feeling of unfamiliarity and a moment of disorientation. Too often the first inclination is to fill the gap with some kind of commotion, even though, as the quote above indicates, we often profess to yearn for peace and quiet.

It is very easy for me to recall times that I have filled in these awkward moments, these from-to's, with an activity that distracts me from what is going on. Invariably I regret it.

Today I encourage you simply to sit through whatever period of transition you are going through. Stay there a moment. Notice what is going on for you, acknowledge the disorientation and bring all your attention to the present. For instance, arriving home after work, instead of racing in the door, turning on the radio, and picking up the phone, just stay in your car (or on the front step, just outside the front door) for two minutes. The world will not collapse if you take two minutes.

Now you will better know what you need, and how you want to deal with this new time in your life, and you'll be a little more prepared to cope with the new state of being.

We yearn for a moment's peace and quiet, only to turn on the radio, make a phone call, or run an errand as soon as an opportunity for solitude presents itself.

—Ronnie Polanezcky

Today notice your moments of peace, and if your impulse is to fill them.

Gaze Out the Window

So many influences of contemporary life seem to militate against our remaining awake and aware of what is meaningful to us. So much seems to clamor for our attention and keep us from being present to the moment. Everything seems to shout, "Look at me!" or worse, "Look at me right now!"

As an antidote to those demands of life, I invite you to stand and stare, or simply to gaze. Perhaps gaze out the window right now and allow whatever is in your field of vision simply to be there. (Lacking a window, simply gaze about you.) Just let your gaze fall easily upon what is outside the window or what is around you for a moment. Most likely, what you see is ordinary to you; you've seen it many times.

Now notice what is there. Noticing brings you from the general view of gazing to a more specific way to see. You note the weather or the temperature. You notice the time of day and the light. You take note of the things or people within your vision.

Now allow your noticing to call you to a quiet moment. Is the weather cool? What does cool weather lead you to? Is the sun shining? Who is the light of your life? Are we in spring? Is there something budding in your life? Is it a morning scene? What do you want to feel at day's end?

When one of life's voices rudely shouts at you, "Look at me!" respond by standing and staring or with an easy gaze out the window. Then notice the ordinary but noble things you see there.

There are so many opportunities for standing and staring, for gazing and noticing.

What is life if, full of care, We have no time to stand and stare?

—W. H. Davies

Today begin a new custom: Gaze out the window and notice. . . .

41

Quieting Your Day

A great way to become open, and stay open, is simply to be quiet and receptive to what might be:

Be still.
Breathe.
Relax.
Breathe again.
And again.
Let a little time pass, doing nothing.

Slowly the space you are in becomes open, receptive. Slowly, you realize that you can trust the quiet, nothing will scare or overwhelm you. Slowly you begin to realize that this is a time of receiving, not just of emptying. Slowly.

Now again:

Be still.
Breathe.
Relax.
Breathe again.
And again.
Let a little time pass, doing nothing.

Now note how you are feeling at the end of that little practice. Give the feeling a name, like Tranquillity or Composure. And when the time comes for you to get going again, bring Tranquillity or Composure with you. Name it to yourself from time to time during the day and revisit the feeling.

Silence is a receptive space.

—**Barbara De Angelis**

Do this a few times today.

four

Finding Your Balance

Balance

The more I age, the more I know that the spiritual path—life viewed primarily through the prism of our meanings and values—must involve paradox, confusion, dead ends, and shadowed places that are often foul to behold. Any path that tries to avoid these will get us into trouble.

As tempting as it may be, a life lived as if all were beautiful and happy—or could be, if only we knew just how to do it!—is a life doomed either to much unnecessary frustration or to ineffective and lightweight surface skimming.

In the summer, there are always the seeds of winter. When you're down, up will come. In the joy of success dwell the seeds of failure. In moments of bleakest grief shines the light of new energy and life. The dark and the bright, the joyful and the sad, the pleasure and the pain, life and death, death and resurrection.

Now please don't count me among those who don't like to emphasize the good and the happy aspects of life. I was raised, after all, on Johnny Mercer singing, "You gotta ac-*cennn*-tuate the positive, e-*limmm*-inate the negative . . . and don't mess with Mister In-between!"

Isn't the goal to embrace life *just as it really is?* And for that we need time of quiet, time with nothing to distract us, time for just being in the moment. Otherwise we may give in to avoiding or denying anything that we don't find easy or happy.

In the depths of winter, I finally learned that within me there lay an invincible summer.

—Albert Camus

Today, look for the summer in your winter (or the winter in your summer).

Mowing the Lawn

I was a guest author on a National Public Radio program and in the course of our conversation the interviewer said to me: "Let me tell you why I don't get one of those big sit-down lawn mowers, but keep my old small one. First, it uses less gas, but really it's because when I am walking behind my old lawn mower, I am in a different space. For some reason I just feel different—quiet, peaceful—and I like it."

I'm glad he didn't let anyone talk him into getting a new lawn mower. Walking along behind his lawn mower is his time of serenity, his quiet time—yes, even with the lawn mower's racket—his time for himself, and his over-busy life does not allow for much of it.

Often, we do in fact have times of quiet and peace, times of doing nothing, but we just don't identify them as such. It helps to identify them, because then we will value them more clearly and defend them more staunchly. What are those times for you? Swimming laps? Doing dishes? Digging in the garden? The more we recognize how we find those times of peace and serenity already in our lives, the more we can be conscious in choosing them.

And remember to look for your serenity where you might not expect to find it, like walking along behind a noisy mower.

Everyone thinks I'm crazy not to get a sit-down mower.

—radio host

Today notice some valued, but previously unidentified, times of doing nothing.

46

A Walk Down the Street

I took a walk down my street yesterday and noticed a few things:

There are those two very yellow houses right next to each other, the only yellow houses on the block.

The elms are not showing the slightest bit of green and here it's already the middle of April.

There goes the woman who runs with wolves, a serious runner accompanied by four equally serious wolves, although they are probably wolflike dogs. I enjoy her energy.

Just noticing various things as you walk down your street can be more powerful than it might seem. The noticing—paying attention to what you see, hear, feel, taste, and smell—brings you into the present time and place and takes you out of worry, planning, and anxiety.

As I return to my work I feel refreshed, renewed.

Walking is treading upon the Earth. Thus I remember my humanity, my place on the Earth, my belonging. I imagine the curve of the Earth and the small part of the curve I traverse.

I have also noticed that my walking brings me some practical benefits. Sometimes an image of what I recently noticed on my walk will be just what I needed as a symbol or metaphor for what I am trying to express. The yellow houses in fact reminded me of something that I had meant to do recently but had forgotten.

For the most part, however, just walk. The rest will take care of itself.

> I took a walk on Spaulding's farm the other afternoon. I saw the setting sun lighting up the opposite side of a stately pine wood.
>
> **—Henry David Thoreau**

> Walk down your street today. What do you notice?

47

Really Nothing New

At the end of one of my seminars, I was about to thank people for coming and ask if there were any more questions or ideas. There seemed to be none so I had begun to say good-night when from the very back of the room I caught a glimpse of someone waving a hand tentatively. Even from a distance, I could tell it was a hand that had seen many seasons.

I acknowledged the wave, "Yes, someone in the back?"

Very slowly an old man came out from his seat into the aisle and walked a little way toward the front. He was smiling.

"I have enjoyed your talk," he said, "and what you say is most important, but it is really nothing new. When I was a boy in Italy I learned the importance of one of our favorite sayings: *Dolce far niente.* How sweet it is to do nothing."

He paused, then said it again, slowly, with a great deal of feeling, and a strong, careful gesture, making it obvious that he not only believed it, but had lived it: *"Dolce far niente!"*

Certainly, the idea of intentionally spending deliberate time doing nothing in order to find peace and serenity is nothing new. It is part of literally every major religious and spiritual tradition, as well as often a part of many national and regional cultures. I particularly like the Italian one mentioned here. In just three beautiful words there is such joy and feeling.

Dolce far niente!

—old Italian saying

Can you identify a part of one of your traditions— religious, ethnic, cultural, linguistic— that encourages doing nothing on purpose?

Simplifying Prayer

The simpler, the more complete? Rodin's words become clearer, more powerful, when you think of his sculptures—*The Thinker*, for example, or his portrayal of John the Baptist. The simple, clear, strong lines, free of much fine detail, capture an essence.

So many of us stay away from prayer because we are convinced that we don't really know how to do it, or there are certain ways it should be done, or certain results should occur, or only certain kinds of believing people should pray.

But prayer is simply an attitude of the heart that desires communication with the divine, however it is found. It is utterly simple. Both for those who think and pray in terms of a specific God as well as for those who don't, prayer informs and transforms our lives.

Consider:

Who changes with prayer? Is it not the one praying?

Why pray? Is it not, like in any relationship, to be in touch?

Is one type of prayer better than another type? Or is it a question of how do I need to pray right now?

Is there any right way to pray? Any wrong way?

Prayer is an attitude of the heart. It can be expressed in myriad ways. There is no limit. There are no boundaries. We must not worry at all about the details of prayer, but only the essence of connecting. Let go of concern about how well or how long or how wisely you pray.

Kahlil Gibran reminds us, "There is a desire within us that drives [us]. . . to the divine." Allow the desire to have its way, to be in control, to lead you to new ways to pray.

The simpler the prayer, the more complete.

The more simple we are, the more complete we become.

—attributed to
August Rodin

Notice today how often you are, indeed, praying.

Still Life

Columnist and theologian Smith was hoping for some snow. As for many of us, the holidays are wonderful for her, but too often they become the "get ready, get set, GO holidays." And now, the holidays over, she faced: "Schedules. Deadlines. Carpools. Too much to do and not enough time to do it in." What she needed was some snow.

One evening she and her children prayed for snow; the children wanted school canceled, she wanted life to be still.

"[The next] morning met us with wonder. It stopped us in our tracks. Its beauty took our breath away. Everything dusted in white. . . . Everything quiet. . . . Snow is spread out like an endless blanket . . . wrapping us all in the welcome gift of 'Just Stop.' Just stop rushing. Just stop racing. Just stop running from one thing to another. Slow down. Let go. Breathe. And Just Stop. Just Be. Be still. Be quiet. Be.

"And so, we did. We had no choice. Which is sometimes the best choice of all."

Before the snow, Smith was feeling the effects of the "hard days" of the give and take of family life when, "We forget who we are. Who we are supposed to be. . . . Sometimes we even unravel. We wonder: Will we ever be whole again? . . . In the dead of winter, I'd been longing for life, 'Still Life.'"

What can be "snow" for you today? Watch for opportunities to stop and play with people you love and whose company you enjoy. And make it a rule: When something is canceled, rained out, or snowed in, seek your Still Life.

In the dead of winter, I'd been longing for Life, Still Life.

—Eileen Smith

Look for "snow" today and discover your Still Life.

In the Sunshine

Read Helen Keller's words again. What do they mean to you? I am fond of this aphorism because it seems to me that it can mean two very different—maybe even opposing—things. Let me paraphrase each one.

First interpretation: Keep looking on the bright side of life, emphasizing the positive, and then you will not even notice the negative and painful parts in the shadow. If you keep your face toward the welcome sun, you won't even notice the unwelcome shadow.

Second interpretation: Watch out, because if you only see the bright side of things, you will miss the dark side, which can then do you harm. If you only look at the sunny side, you'll miss what the shadow side has to offer you.

Here is an opportunity to practice both/and rather than either/or. We don't have to affirm one and deny the other. We can use either, both, or neither.

There are days I need the sunshiny encouragement of the first interpretation, and other days I need the shadowy warning of the second. There are whole periods of life when I need one more than the other. There are also times with neither one hits me as significant.

Which of the two truths is best for you right now? Or do you need them both, but in different parts of your life? Or not at all?

Keep your face to the sunshine and you cannot see the shadow.

—attributed to
Helen Keller

Today, notice
the sunshine,
notice the shadow.
Which do you
need more now?

Curbing Forgetfulness

There is a secret bond between slowness and memory, between speed and forgetting.

—**Milan Kundera**

What strikes me when I read Kundera's quote is the word *secret*. These are secret bonds. With some moments of reflection, the truth of the whole statement is fairly evident, but why are these bonds secret?

My guess is that they are secret because we have not noticed them before. As recently as a generation ago, these bonds were a common, intuitive understanding. People lived their lives with a conscious realization of the balance between slowness and remembering, between speed and forgetting. They knew that leisure was a necessary part of a balanced life. They knew that if you moved too fast you were bound to forget something.

We know it too, but only if we stop to recollect it. Contemporary life does not afford us the intuitive awareness of our forebears. It is, in fact, counterintuitive to a life in balance. Unthinking acceptance of our culture's rate of speed is a terrible, yet common, error. These formerly secret bonds must now be noticed with full intention, and more, shouted from the rooftops.

If we don't notice the bond between speed and forgetting, we will forget what we need to remember. And we will constantly wonder why life is not working out the way we wanted it to, or why we are always seeking inner peace and not finding it.

One of the secrets about forgetting: You forget that you forgot.

> No matter what today's schedule is, don't forget Stillpoints. They curb forgetfulness.

Soulbody

Why are we so reluctant to make the connections between the mind and the body? Certainly one of the reasons is that for centuries our Western institutional churches have separated them. I learned very early that I had a soul, and that it could be marked, and that the soul was important and good. And I had a body that was different, less important; it somehow contained the soul. Today I would rather say we are not a soul in a body, nor a body in a soul. We're soulbody.

The underlying assumption in separating and distinguishing the soul from the body is to see the soul as spiritual, good, and eternal. It is separated from the body, which is physical, not so good (maybe even bad), and dies. Ultimately this splitting has put us at war with ourselves.

I have a theory that responds in a very practical way to this unhealthy splitting: When you are experiencing physical malady, it is an indication of spiritual disquiet, and thus its treatment must be spiritual. Conversely, when you are aware of a spiritual malaise, it is a sign that some physical reality needs healing and thus the treatment will be in the bodily realm.

Thus, for a headache, instead of popping pills, take the afternoon off. And for anxiety, rather than a therapy session, get thee to the gym.

The theory can, of course, be carried too far. Aspirin can relieve a headache, and therapy anxiety. But more of a problem is that we don't use the theory at all.

Try it to see if it works for you.

All the soarings of my mind begin in my blood.

—**Rainer Maria Rilke**

Today: Identify a physical ill and a spiritual healing, or a spiritual ill and a physical healing.

five

The Moments in Between

Dental Hygiene

All of us have the space-in-between of teethbrushing. For a moment, bring to mind the times that you brush your teeth. Maybe it's twice a day, in the morning and before bed. If you're really good, it's after every meal. Perhaps occasionally at work.

What are you thinking about as you brush your teeth?

Buddhists remind us, when you brush your teeth, just brush your teeth. Be mindful. Be aware of who you are and what you're doing just now.

My mother's advice, when I was just learning the importance of dental hygiene, was this: "Always brush your teeth for the length of five Hail Marys, and don't rush them."

By my quick calculations, if we spend a minute twice a day—using my mother's Hail Mary standard—by the age of forty we will have already spent about 486 hours, or twenty days, brushing our teeth.

Imagine all those hours filled with intentional mindful breathing, or gentle remembering, or praying, rather than just mindless, impatient scrubbing.

Avoid not only false teeth, but also false life.

Be true to your teeth or your teeth will be false to you.
—**dental proverb**

Beginning today, bring meaning as well as brushing to your dental hygiene.

Grand Central Station

My aunt was fond of saying—and I particularly remember her saying it during the family-filled times of Christmas—"It looks like Grand Central Station in here!" She was referring to the hustle and bustle that are the result of the comings and goings of many people in a given place, in this case, our overfull living room.

Grand Central Station in New York has become an American icon of a crowded and busy place, with many people coming and going. Hardly a place for recollection, quietude, or serenity. And yet....

Serenity is available anywhere you seek it.

The author quoted above is a contemporary writer who was researching the recent renovations of the famed rail terminal and it was there, in the middle of that "frenetic public space," that he did feel "oddly serene." Perhaps he added "oddly" because the serenity was so unexpected.

As you find yourself in busy, public places that bustle with activity, let the contrast between what is going on and what you seek, between frenzy and peace, be your guide to serenity. Be still, while all about you swirl the comings and goings of the world.

What are your bustling places? Maybe a transportation terminal, sports stadium, or shopping mall? Or maybe your family room or your kitchen? Wherever they are, let the frenzy call you to the inner serenity that is accessible in any moment.

In the middle of this famously frenetic public space, I find myself feeling oddly serene.

—**David Michaelis**

Identify a frenetic place in your day and find your own odd serenity there.

Wild Places

And, I might add, the nearer, the dearer—at least as far as making the wilderness accessible to as many people as possible. We are used to hearing that the wilderness is dear: "Save the rain forests!" Are we used to hearing that it's often near too?

Those who visit present-day Walden Pond in Concord, Massachusetts, where Thoreau spent his two years in contemplation and solitude, are often struck by how civilized the area has become; it's in the middle of busy communities.

In fact, Walden Pond was not really wilderness even when Thoreau lived there. He writes about visitors, and of hearing wagons on the road, and of going to the village for supplies.

Walden was a wilderness within reach. We have them too: Greenbelts along our rivers, parks in our cities and counties, lake and ocean shores, reservoirs with adjacent park land, trails through woods or forests. All of these are places that can lead us, as Walden did Thoreau, to quietude, to peacefulness, and thus to keeping our priorities clear and our lives on track.

We don't have to trek off to some remote part of the Earth to arrive at the state of wilderness. It is anywhere we come in touch with the peace and beauty of the natural world.

The Sea of Cortez or the community park—the soul can soar in both.

The wilderness is near as well as dear.

—**Henry David Thoreau**

Today identify your close wilderness and make a note to visit soon.

Daily Shower

I think some resourceful parent must have invented that saying to shame children into taking a bath, because I've known some less-than-clean folk who seemed well in tune with the divine.

If this saying were indeed and literally true, we would be a very godly nation, for God knows, we're a clean one. And yet, the saying lasts; it must have truth.

However, whether you take a bath or a shower, whether it's in the morning or in the evening, the moments of cleaning oneself are wonderful for a Stillpoint. Most often bathing is a very personal, intimate, and solitary ritual and thus is a natural time to become more awake and call to mind what you need for the day ahead. It might go something like this:

Close your eyes and take some time just to feel the water on your body. Note its temperature, just how it feels. Notice what else you're feeling.

Breathe deeply one, two, three times, slowly.

As your physical energy is aware of the water, at the same time allow your spiritual energy to turn inward. Both movements are part of the same you, and happen in the same moment.

Let the unwelcome effects of the past day wash off your soul just as its physical residue washes off your body.

Let your spirit be refreshed with the cool, clean water of grace just as the warm, clean water brings relaxation and rejuvenation to your body.

You bring to mind those whom you will likely encounter today, and you recall from the past those who would be your models.

Maybe that saying is truer than I thought.

Cleanliness is next to Godliness.

—**proverb**

Today, try a Shower Stillpoint.

A Warm Cup of...

Is there anything so welcoming, so promising, so inviting to relaxation as being greeted by, say, a beloved old aunt with the words, "Why, come right in, dear, and I'll fix you a nice cup of tea!" It just seems to say, well, things are not so bad after all.

What is it about taking a cup of warm liquid, whether alone or with someone? It is a quiet and intimate gesture in some ways, and yet one that is allowed almost any time and with almost anyone.

Coffee, tea, chocolate? It makes no difference, although, as Emerson suggests, they do have a different feel to them. "The morning cup of coffee has an exhilaration about it which the cheering influence of the afternoon or evening cup of tea cannot be expected to reproduce." Well, maybe.

Morning or afternoon, coffee or tea, alone or with a friend, taking a warm cup of something calls us to reflect, to remember, perhaps to share.

The next time you're frustrated with work, don't just grin and bear it, take a moment and enjoy a cup of tea. Pay attention to the tea ritual, even if it is only with a tea bag and a paper cup.

When you find yourself discouraged by your slow progress with a project, seize the would-be moment of gloom and treat yourself to a five-minute coffee break. Notice the taste and warmth of the coffee. Pay attention to it. Only then return to your project.

Out of sorts? Feeling cranky? Instead of playing victim, play host or hostess. Invite someone, anyone—the next-door neighbor, the worker in the next cubicle—for a cup of tea.

Tea! thou soft, thou sober, sage, and venerable liquid . . . thou smile-smoothing, heart-opening, wink-tippling cordial. . . .

—Colley Cibber

Today:
a warm cup of . . .

Flying

These are the first and last lines of a remarkable poem, "High Flight," written on the back of a letter to his parents by a pilot in the Royal Canadian Air Force who perished in World War II.

It is a reminder that flying is the perfect time for reflection:

The exhilaration of speeding down the runway to takeoff and soaring into flight! It's an occasion that can always cause you wonder.

From up here you have a totally different perspective. What seemed to be important a while ago now, from this point of view, seems less so. Other parts of life loom larger and more urgent.

At 30,000 feet and 600 miles an hour, you feel on the edge of the universe. Almost a space traveler. God seems closer.

Flying indeed is the perfect time to come back to ourselves. In fact, it's hard to image a better opportunity. And the metaphors and imagery suggested by flying support a poetic and spiritual moment.

The next time you're in flight, before you take out the laptop, before you reach for the cell phone, before you open your book, look out the window or into your soul, or both.

You too just might touch the face of God.

> *Oh! I have slipped the surly bonds of Earth . . . and touched the face of God.*
>
> **—John G. Magee, Jr.**

The next time you fly, or see a plane flying, reflect. . . .

La Bella Luna

If there is one symbol that more than any other calls human beings to a moment of stillness and reflection, it must be the moon.

Which of us cannot identify many moments in our lives when we noticed the moon, made a comment on its particular way of being out this night, and thus brought ourselves, and perhaps those with us, to a moment of transcendence?

Moonstruck is a happy movie about an Italian family in Brooklyn. The beautiful moon, *la bella luna,* is a symbol that runs through the story and calls each of the main characters to a moment of quiet reflection, and thus to a deeper recognition of their love.

The above dialogue is between Loretta (played by Cher) and Ronnie (Nicholas Cage) and is a moment of recognition for them.

Everyone in the film has pain and hurt with which they struggle, sometimes without a lot of success. The moon is the silent witness to all of their lives. The moon seems to say, by its simple and mysterious presence, that there is more to life than sometimes it seems, there are some people you can indeed trust, and it's important to follow your heart.

But first you have to notice it. You have to spend some time looking at the moon—or perhaps howling at it—in order for it to call you to a moment of reflection and insight.

Anticipate your next encounter with *la bella luna.* Determine to allow it to bring you to a moment of quiet contemplation.

RONNIE: *What's the matter?*

LORETTA: *Nothing, I'm looking at the moon. I never seen a moon like that before.*

RONNIE: *Makes you look like an angel.*

—**from** *Moonstruck*

Tonight, look for the moon.

Still Time

Yes, I am also convinced that time can stand still. I believe, in fact, that this stopped time is the most real time of all. The Irish writer John Banville, in his novel *The Untouchable*, describes the desire of one of his characters to tell his listener about the really "true things":

"I wanted to tell her about the blade of sunlight cleaving to the velvet shadows . . . of the incongruous gaiety of the rain shower that fell the day of my father's funeral, of that night . . . when I saw the red ship under the Blackfriars Bridge and conceived of the tragic significance of my life: in other words, the real things; the true things."

These are the moments when time stands still. Sunlight, a rain shower, and a red ship are symbols that carry meaning. But Banville's character's heart holds "the real things." His inner life was more urgently meaningful than the externals about which he will actually speak: why he was in the sunlight at that moment, with whom he was walking when he saw the red ship, even his father's funeral.

When time stands still, you can be sure that something very important is leaping in.

To allow this pregnant calm, we must be still, like a leaf slowly turning and turning on a stream, caught in an eddy, while the stream continues its fall to the sea.

Watch for your time-standing-still moments as you go about your busy days. What are they like for you? Can you recall some from your past?

And especially, watch for the truth. Pay a lot of attention to the truth that leaps in at those moments, for it will surely enrich your life.

Time can stand still,
I am convinced of it;
something snags and stops,
turning and turning,
like a leaf on a stream.

—John Banville

What will help you notice time standing still?

A Living Picture

Do you feel the full impact of that statement? It is really quite a remarkable thing to say. A picture *lives* by companionship? Unfeeling eyes can hurt it? These are words of one who lives in the world of paradox and mystery, below the surface, in the spirit world, the most real and certainly the most interesting of all the worlds.

One of my deep convictions is that we need to pay more attention to artists. They reflect and interpret our world. They see what the rest of us are too busy, too distracted, or otherwise incapable of seeing. They say to us simply: Look at this! Take some time and see this! It's important!

Too often we dismiss artists as temperamental and difficult and even as unwilling to get a "real" job. Except for the very few who become trendy and collectable in their lifetimes, most die poor. The great ones make money for heirs and collectors.

It is not surprising that the words above come from the twentieth-century painter, Mark Rothko. Born in Russia, he lived and worked in America. He is a color-field painter of the abstract expressionist school. His late and most recognized works are huge canvases of softly painted or blurred blocks of color, often dark, which seem to float in front of another colored ground. If you stand quietly before one in a museum long enough, you will probably hear some comments which indicate that the art is challenging to the viewer. Some words might be statements of the "unfeeling" that can "impair" the work.

I'm not sure I understand or even appreciate Rothko's work, but I try to remember his words so as not to hurt his picture with my eyes.

A picture lives by companionship. It dies by the same token. It is therefore risky to send it out into the world. How often it must be impaired by the eyes of the unfeeling.

—Mark Rothko

Next time you visit a museum, be aware of your power.

six
Creating Opportunities for Serenity

Writing

By its nature, writing slows you down. With pencil and pad relaxing on your sofa, or with laptop at 30,000 feet and supersonic speed, writing focuses your attention, stills your soul.

But is it, as the learned lord suggests, a way to learn? If so, what can be learned from writing? I can't answer for Lord Acton, but I know some of the ways it works for me.

When I write, I must go more deeply in search and exploration of myself. Thus I learn, more than anything, about me.

Learn as much by writing as by reading.
—Lord Acton

When I write, I must continually research the material. Thus I learn about the world.

When I write, I pursue the appropriate word to use, with the precise meaning I need. I want to find the exact brocard, craft the precise zeugma.

When you write in a diary or in a journal, who knows what will pop out of your pen? Sometimes you don't realize what you have written until, perhaps months later, you return to read it. *I wrote that?*

Write poetry. It allows you to express feelings and ideas that otherwise might not have been born. Refine and revise your poems until they are most pleasing to you. No need to worry about publication.

Write letters. Especially these days, a handwritten letter says that you took extra time and special effort. Write e-mails. Write postcards to friends. Write notes to yourself.

Determine to spend time today writing something.

Write stories. Write essays. As you let the world hear from you, you'll probably hear from the world in some way.

Write anything, and learn much.

The Singer, Not the Song

Why does the spiritual teacher encourage us to sing? Isn't it because there is nothing quite so effective as singing to get what is inside of you out? Nothing better expresses your feelings and attitudes to the world, whether or not any of the world is hearing it.

The point is not the hearing; it's the singing.

Singing creates a habit of moving inner feelings to accessibility, to a place where other people can share them. And in order to move them out, you have to encounter them, forge them into words and melody, and send them forth in all their harmony and beauty. Or in all their off-key cacophony. No matter.

When we are awake to the moment, when we are aware of ourselves, when we remember who we are, we will sing: a melancholy ballad, a soaring saraband, or a droning dirge; it depends on what is inside. Sing in the shower as you prepare for the day, in the car as you drive home from work, during your morning walk. Sing to your children, or with them.

One of the reasons I love musicals—that most American expression of theater—is the way the characters, in an unselfconscious and unlikely way, burst out into song at all the right moments. Maybe we all would love the freedom to do that.

Even if you can't sing well, sing. Sing to yourself. Sing in the privacy of your own home. But sing.

—Rebbe Nachman

Sometime today:
Stop and sing!
Out loud!

Books

That's a statement of a person with a passion. It's easy to understand not being able to live without food or water or even companionship, but books? Yes, books!

Oh, Jefferson would no doubt have continued to live without them, he probably wouldn't really have died, but neither would he have been as fully alive as he wanted to be.

Of the many gifts of the world that can lead us to contemplation, to creative reverie, to quiet moments of being in the present, perhaps books are the most powerful. Or am I just revealing my own biased attraction to Jefferson's words?

My father used to love to say to someone who had just given him a book as a gift, "Oh, that's too bad, I already have a book!" as if it were a duplicate of a necktie.

His humor got at a deeper truth: you really can't have too many books. They hold the world for our perusal.

I have a list of special books. Currently it contains five titles. I call it my life-changing book list. Each of these volumes has undeniably changed the way I live. The first title on the list is *Stuart Little* by E.B. White. In truth, the list could contain all the books I have ever read, for they have all changed my life in some way.

What are some significant books in your life?

Imagine yourself with one of them, seated in your favorite chair, the book held loosely in your lap, staring into space in contemplation of something the writer has just suggested to you, and which you are now following in your own reverie....

> *I cannot live without books.*
>
> —**Thomas Jefferson**

Spend some time with a favorite book today.

A Place at Home

This is from *Metropolitan Home?* Yes, it appears in an introduction to one of their home-of-the-month articles, which features a meditation room designed on the ancient principles of feng shui, the Chinese art of arranging things in your home based on spiritual principles.

It's another example of how desperately we all need to find serenity in our lives. "And this need for reflection, for quality down-time," say the editors, "applies equally to living rooms and bedrooms, kitchens and baths. People have long been devoted to their homes; what we have begun to see are homes that are themselves devotional."

We all have need for sacred space. Churches and synagogues and mosques are sacred spaces for many people. And certainly a place for quiet moments or for meditation is not new to many homes, although most will not have a separate room dedicated exclusively to that purpose as does the magazine's featured home.

In many cultures, homes have what might be described as a shrine, or a devotional place with meaningful sacred symbols.

My own shrine is simply the corner of a bookshelf. It holds symbols of life for me. Among them are nails from a torn-down building, a family medal, a Costa Rican cross, and a replica of a Haida totem.

Think of your own home. Is there a place there that calls you, and those with whom you live, to be still, to be quiet? Having such a space is important, for when you go there, you are immediately surrounded by a feeling that you want to go in.

People are feeling a need to sit still, to breathe, to take a pause in their daily routine.

—from *Metropolitan Home* **magazine**

If there is a devotional place in your home, enjoy it today. If not, would you create one?

The Sentences

About a year ago, I decided that my exposure to the great works of world literature was too limited, so I began to go back, so to speak, and catch up. Why I decided to begin with Proust, the French novelist, is anyone's guess.

But that's where I began, and that's where I am still, creeping my way through *Swann's Way,* the first of the seven volumes of his epic novel *Remembrance of Things Past.*

The creeping is not because it is dull, which it rarely is, although it can be slow moving; nor is it because the writing is complex; that too is characteristic. It is because of the sentences. Oh, the sentences!

I have never read such sentences. They can go on forever and ever, sometimes taking up the whole page. And they contain entire worlds of feeling, and nuanced insights into human behavior, and observation of life. So I read them over and over. That's why I'm creeping. It just takes me a long time to read, and then re-read, all those improbable sentences.

The snippet quoted above is from one of them, one of my favorites. It is fully half a page long, and it describes not something that happened in his life, but something that might have happened, had a few other things occurred as well.

Why, I ask myself, do I read these boulderlike sentences over and over again?

I read them over and over because they make me still. At least that's one of their effects. There are others.

. . . and the passerby, should he turn round to make sure that I have not gone astray, may be amazed to see me still standing there . . . gazing at the steeple for hours on end. . . .

—**Marcel Proust**

Think of some reading that makes you still, centered, or quiet.
Take it from the shelf today.

Nature as Therapist

Afellow psychotherapist and I have often joked that when the weather turns warm and balmy in the spring, we seem to have fewer new clients and more appointment cancellations, whereas the cold and dark months of winter bring a greater number of ardent seekers to our doors.

Nature indeed is a good therapist. So make an appointment with what drives the foolishness out of you.

Is it the wind blowing strong in your face as you stand on the ocean shore or mountaintop, cleaning out, as it were, the old, gathered cobwebs of pain or sadness?

The sun? It warms your back as you take a walk in the morning, inviting you into the day, and assuring you that all is right in the heavens.

The rain? In spritzes or in torrents, it brings life to our Earth, food to our tables, and a feeling of closeness and security when seen through the window of a dry and warm home.

Clouds? Always changing and moving and sometimes totally absent or represented by the merest waft, they are always taking the shapes of things or reminding us of something. And they never fail to uplift the spirit.

And Nature is almost always accessible. In cities and office buildings look for plants and indoor trees to spend a moment with, windows with views of the sky, a nearby city park or greenbelt where you can pause and refresh, drive out the foolishness, and return to life.

There is nothing so good as the wind and the sun for driving the foolishness out of one.

—**Roycroft Epigrams,**
1923

Today, make an appointment for a therapy session with Nature.

Monastics

Monasteries and convents are where men and women go to be monastics, to live the quiet life of prayer, simplicity, and work in a community of the like-minded.

But many men and women who live in the larger world, with relationships, families, careers, and friends, are successful in bringing parts of the monastic life into their secular routines.

Dennis is a professional health care provider, with a spouse and a full life of patients and teaching. But he also finds time for meditation, a daily horarium of prayer, and several spaces of quiet contemplation. He used to be a monk in a monastery; now he's a "monk" in his home and office.

Patricia is a nurse. She leads a very quiet but full life of service, working at the hospital, and volunteering much time to community projects that serve children. Her day is built upon a structure of prayer and quietude. This is her life of choice. Her husband, of a similar inclination, often joins her.

Lisa is an artist. She spends most of her day in her studio painting, which for her is a spiritual practice. She lives alone and has an active social life with family members, friends, and colleagues.

It is clear that the people mentioned here have made the monastic part of their lives a priority and thus have chosen to forgo other aspects. Most of us are not in a position to make such a choice. Two of those described above are parents but none have children living at home.

Even if your circumstances are different, is there a way, even a small way, you would like to express the monastic hidden in you?

'Tis not the habit that makes the monk.

—Thomas Fuller

Today, reflect on the possibility of monastic moments.

Staying Home

Some reflections on staying home:

Home alone! I feel lucky when I have my home to myself for a while.

"A place you don't have to deserve." That's how poet Robert Frost refers to home.

It seems to me a feeling of safety should exist in my home. I shouldn't have to be vigilant there.

Some questions about staying home:

Do you have real comfort in your home? How can you make your home more inviting for you to stay there more often? Paint the walls a new color? Find a comfortable, well-lighted place to read? Is there the degree of order and neatness you need?

No time alone? See if you can come up with times when no one else is around, early in the morning maybe.

No space to separate from spouse, kids, housemates? Can you designate a room as a place apart where one can go and be allowed to be alone?

What will I do if I just stay home? Fuss around. Look through drawers. Write a letter or two. Browse books. Bake a cake. Take a walk. Balance the checkbook. Make a phone call. Read a poem. Write a poem. Sit still.

Yes, there is a lot to do out there, many cultural attractions, or many naturally beautiful places to visit. They'll always be there, or others like them, or better ones.

But it's Saturday night and everyone is out having fun!

Yes, and you are staying home and having fun.

There is nothing like staying home for real comfort.

—Jane Austen

Today, make plans to stay home for real comfort.

You've Gotta Have Art!

If everyday serenity were to have a patron artist, I am aware of none more suitable than Jan Vermeer, a Dutch painter who lived and worked in Delft in the mid-seventeenth century. "Vermeer's genius was in probing those moments when one feels alone and immersed in one's thoughts," notes art historian A.K. Wheelock.

Perhaps you recall seeing his well-known *Young Woman with a Water Jug.* It portrays a woman—she wears a nunlike head and shoulder covering—one hand on a water pitcher, the other reaching toward a window, which casts light and shadow upon her as she gazes into mid-space. The artist captures her in this moment of reflection, of contemplation.

Many of Vermeer's paintings capture individuals, mostly women, most often in the light of a window, in these moments of reverie, of dream-like trance, of contemplation.

The *Young Woman,* like all of Vermeer's paintings, makes it easy to know that he tendered a deep love for the part of the world he painted. And it gets me wondering...

What is the woman pondering? What has captured her inner attention so? Has she thought of someone? A memory? There's a slight smile on her face; is she in a light mood, about to laugh? Or is she just pausing, enjoying the peace of the moment?... until I too am still.

What art speaks to you of deep love of the world? Brings you to a moment of quiet contemplation?

To give a list of the great artists that the world has seen would be to name a list of lovers.

—Roycroft Epigrams,
1923

Today find a work of art that leads you to stillness, to contemplation.

Trees

Is there a better place than among trees to sit still? They seem to foster stillness, quietude, and reverie.

Think of the trees you have known, specific ones that you remember from past times and places, or those in your life now, perhaps right outside your window. Reflect on them for a moment....

Here are snippets from my reverie:

In the backyard of my childhood home in Ohio was a flowering plum with dark red leaves and rough, dark-gray bark, growing next to the garage. I would run toward it at breakneck speed, grab onto its lowest limb, swing up to the next, then up to the next, now bracing my foot on an awkwardly protruding branch which had a little give to it, which would push me to the last limb and thus to my destination, the "porch" on top of the garage. The journey was one flowing movement, ground to roof, the plum tree the vehicle. We ate the plums too. The flowering plum outside my window now looks nothing like the other one, but it reminds me....

Two giant... were they oaks? maples? Grew so close together that my grandfather put up a swing between them with long ropes stretching far up the towering trunks. We would swing for hours....

It was a delicate palm tree, just the right size. We saw it beside the road in Cali, Colombia, and quickly agreed with the owner on a price. We dug it up and took it home and planted it in the living room, which was, in that climate, partially open to the sky. The little palm thrived, contrary to all predictions. I wonder, is it still there...?

Trees can make you still; stillness can bring memories... climbing, swinging, planting....

I go among trees and sit still.

—Wendell Berry

Allow the trees in your life—past and present—to lead you to reverie.

seven

Defining Your Values

Living Spirituality

Spiritual is a difficult word, and for that reason, many people avoid it. Jon Kabat-Zinn's comments are a good expression of this attitude: "As much as I can, I avoid using the word *spiritual* altogether," he says. "I find it neither useful nor necessary nor appropriate.... I have a problem with the inaccurate, incomplete, and frequently misguided connotations of [the] word."

I respect this attitude and, for a while, espoused it. But most people continue to use the words *spiritual* and *spirituality,* and I cannot find others that take their place more effectively. So I (somewhat arbitrarily) assign meaning to the words and thus have come to appreciate and value them.

The meaning of *spirituality* that I choose to embrace—for it is not only my definition—is: the meanings and values by which you live your life, combined with, for believers, the way you experience the divine. The combination of God, meanings, and values is spirituality.

But, of course, this does not exhaust the ways to define it, or indeed the ways to experience it (thus the value of the doubters).

I'm drawn to Brenda Ueland's expression above. The whole quote is: "It is when you are really living in the present—working, thinking, lost, absorbed in something you care about very much, that you are living spiritually." I like that very much. Michelangelo expressed it this way: "It is well with me only when I have a chisel in my hand."

It is exactly during those moments, when your meanings and your values and your awareness of God combine to create the energy that takes charge of your time, that you live life to the fullest.

It is when you are really living in the present . . . that you are living spiritually.

—**Brenda Ueland**

Identify the ways your spirituality is expressed throughout the day.

Bigger: Better or Worse?

The more I give power to the idea that bigger is always better, the more I push out the presence of the smaller, quieter, often spiritual realities that call me to my values.

The more material resources at my disposal, the more difficult it is to acknowledge my lack of control in life, my responsibility in being part of the human community. The more distractions I allow, the less will I notice my chosen spiritual values.

A big house is not a bad thing and a small house is not a good thing. They are just things to be reckoned with, things to be named as powers capable of influencing whether God and spiritual values are in the place you want them.

Many of us live—especially compared to the rest of the world's population—in big houses, meaning we have a having a good number of possessions and resources.

Perhaps this is the reason for the popularity of the idea of simplicity and simple living. Perhaps we are connecting thoughtless accumulation of things with a frustrating—and often fast—life, and simplicity with peace and slowing down.

It is challenging but certainly possible to have a big house with your spiritual priorities in their proper corner. It is also possible to have a small house and God, hat in hand, standing in the hall.

What is the size of your house? Where are your spiritual values?

In a small house God has his corner, in a big house he has to stand in the hall.

—Swedish proverb

Today, consciously bring to mind the size of your house and then notice where God is in it.

The Friend of Silence

For Mother Teresa, activity did not lead to God, silence did. The point to consider is what leads you to an attitude of prayer, to making contact with the divine?

Here are some questions to ponder:

What kind of silence speaks to you of God? There are many kinds of silences. I can imagine that for some, perhaps for you, the roar of the ocean or even the hum of urban noise is a kind of silence that can lead to God. Is it the silence that comes from the tumult of a storm? From the roar of the surf? Or do you prefer the deeper quiet of a forest glade?

Who encourages you to an attitude of silence or prayer? A friend? A saint, officially canonized or not?

Where do you feel most quiet or most open to the divine? At home? In a church? Perhaps a museum or a park?

What are some personal links to prayer? A book or image? A place? Sacred texts?

For Mother Teresa, activity did not lead to God, silence did; but it is also obvious that the God she encountered in silence led her to remarkable activity.

Spending time doing nothing creatively and on purpose, giving your spiritual values opportunity to be present and urgent to you, has the result of prioritizing your whole life. It clarifies and motivates. It can move you to magnificent activity.

[God] cannot be found in noise and restlessness. God is the friend of silence.

—**Mother Teresa of Calcutta**

Today, find some silence in which to spend some moments.

Care

One of the best ways, it seems to me, to determine your spirituality—the meanings and values by which you live—is to ask yourself the question, What do I really care about?

Recently I took some shirts to the laundry, as I do quite regularly. It is a family-run business and over the years I have come to know the family members who work there. This time I noticed a couple of my shirts had buttons missing. The woman who owns the laundry noticed the missing buttons too and offered to replace them. "Wonderful," I said, "Yes, please do."

A week later, when I went to pick up my shirts, I noticed that she had indeed carefully replaced the buttons—matching them exactly—but was not charging me for the work. I called it to her attention. "Oh, no," she said, "I am happy to do it for you."

Her single act of caring made me notice, in that moment, something else about her. She was caring in everything she did: her gestures, her words, her work, her sewing, her counting of the shirts, her handing me the package, her smile, her making change.

I noticed too, from my many brief visits, that she also cared about friendly, competent service, doing more than she was paid to do, being generous, her family.

She is not missing life. "In all the small . . . ways," she cares.

Life is not lost by dying; life is lost minute by minute, day by dragging day, in all the small uncaring ways.

—Stephen Vincent Benét

Look for all your small ways to care today and for the expression of care by others.

Awesome

Awesome! may be the way your teenager responds to what has just pleased her greatly, be it a motorcycle ride, the film she just saw, or even a chocolate chip cookie. (At least, I think they're still using the word.) Even though I sometimes envy teenagers' ability to be amazed by the simple pleasures life has to offer, I prefer Goethe's definition of the word and like to save it for a more deserving occasion.

It is the finest portion we have. Awe is not just an expression of wonder and reverence and respect. In awe, these feelings are mingled with dread or fear, and in its embrace we are aware of the presence of the immense.

The feeling of awe is a sign that we have a certain degree of being awake, aware, and open to the combination of feelings that create it. When we are in its embrace, we tend to be still, silent, observant. Awe is often anticipated and fostered when we are alone and at rest. When awestruck in the presence of other people, each will spend that moment of awe alone, absorbed, riveted by the power. Only later will we share the experience as we reflect on it.

"Make this Bed with Awe—" are the poetic words Emily Dickinson used as she anticipated her death. A deathbed is indeed to be made with awe, for in it we await the immense and "excellent and fair" judgment. What are some other moments when *awesome* is the right word for you? As I think again, I am wondering about the teenager's chocolate chip cookie and motorcycle ride. Could those really be awesome?

Awe is the finest portion of mankind. . . . In awe one feels profoundly the immense.

—Goethe

To what do you truly respond, "Awesome!"

Work and Play

Perhaps this adage grew out of the nineteenth-century Industrial Revolution in England, when many children knew little of play and too much of work. Think of Oliver Twist.

Our own age has nothing to crow about when it comes to balancing work and play—though we're talking about adults now. Ask anyone who works with families—physicians, counselors, nurses, lawyers—workaholism is alive and well, too well. Workaholism is not the same as working hard; it is compulsive, or addictive working; there is a loss of control. And it certainly isn't just Jack that's affected; Jill has long ago joined the ranks of the dull.

Everyone acknowledges the prevalence of workaholism and everyone seems to decry it, and yet we don't attain the balance we say we want. How did we get into such a sorry state?

I wish I had a definitive answer for that. Maybe the answer is very simple: Play more!

Ask yourself some questions to get you going: How do you play? With whom do you play? Do you play at all? Games? Sports? (These are not always play). Have you forgotten how? No problem: just watch children for a while. Then ask to join in.

Also, there is a simple but often overlooked fact: It is extremely difficult to achieve this balance between work and play, given the realities and demands of work and private life. It almost never happens on its own. You have to make it happen in accordance with your values and your priorities, and with purpose and planning. Otherwise, most of the time work wins.

All work and no play make Jack and Jill dull kids.

—traditional saying (adapted)

Play today. Play more all the time. Do you need a plan to make it happen for you?

What Do I Need?

Recently I was in a computer store to buy ink cartridges for my printer. While I was waiting to pay, an enthusiastic clerk was unpacking a brand-new computer for display and was telling me how wonderful this top-of-the-line computer was. Its speed and capacity were state of the art. It left competition in the dust and would give me incredible advantages.

I was hooked. I wanted it. No, I *needed* it, and began to figure out how I could get it.

Later I was telling a friend about the new computer I was going to buy. She said, "Why do you need a new computer?" I answered her question by listing some of the computer's statistics and capacities. "Yes," she said, "but why do you need all that?"

"Why do I need it? Well, I . . . ."

What I really needed was her question. I was asleep, put into a trance by the compelling glitz of something shiny-new. I recognized it in the moment I was unable to answer her with any kind of honest and meaningful response. The truth was, not only did I not need the new computer, I did not even want it. Then how could I have gotten to the point of almost buying it?

It is because an overwhelming number of cultural pressures are exerted upon you and me that tell us we need things we don't need. They are powerful forces. Being awake—and also having awake friends who ask us questions—is the best defense.

Less is more.

—**Robert Browning**

Spend some moments today becoming awake to the difference between things you need and things you don't need.

eight

Paying Attention

Magnificent World

Is there any greater gift than the gift of close attention? Can you recall how you felt on an occasion when the person with whom you were engaged was totally focused on you, eager to know your thoughts, and genuinely interested?

I wonder if you have in such moments the same feeling that I have? When you pay close attention to me, I feel respected. And thus respected, I will do my utmost to make what I am saying or what I am doing the very best it can be. Why? Because I know that you are really listening and taking me seriously.

Your attention calls forth my best efforts.

Close attention is one of the finest gifts we can give our children. It is to them as water and warm sun to a blooming flower. It calls forth their best.

But novelist Henry Miller is taking this a step further. He speaks of paying close attention to a blade of grass, and says that it too will respond by putting forth its best and become "awesome" and "magnificent."

Why not? When you pay attention to me you will see in me what might have, without your attention, remained hidden, even from me. So with a blade of grass: When you pay it attention, you will see what has been there all along, but is now, with the gift of your attention, revealed.

Pay close attention and open an indescribably magnificent world.

The moment one gives close attention to anything, even a blade of grass, it becomes a mysterious, awesome, indescribably magnificent world in itself.

—Henry Miller

> Decide now to whom or to what you will pay close attention today.

The Attentive Heart

The key words in this wise man's teaching are "without your having to force it." What are the manifestations of an attentive heart?

When your heart is attentive you notice what is not there more than what is there, the subtleties more than the obvious.

You notice the quick, wan smile of a friend as she says that everything is fine.

You notice that your colleague is absent from a meeting he always looks forward to.

You notice that when I greeted you this morning I had an expression of unusual joy on my face.

You are aware that your work partner arrives later than usual. You wonder why.

When your heart is attentive you notice the presence of the divine everywhere and all the time, in a handshake, or a smile.

The attentive heart is in love with life and all its expressions and, for the most part, doesn't miss those expressions, no matter how subtle or indirect.

Having an attentive heart is just another name for prayer.

Your heart is attentive, but yearns to be more so. The moments and hours you spend in peaceful quietude are to the heart like moisture and sun to a tree. They transform your heart from the dryness of distraction to the vibrant life of seeing what's truly there, that is, to attention.

It happens on its own, "without your having to force it."

When your heart is attentive, your entire being enters your prayer without your having to force it.

—Rebbe Nachman

Today be conscious of what your heart notices.

A Gift from a Cat

You're walking down the street in your neighborhood and notice a small, black cat several yards ahead of you. She is looking at you.

She doesn't move as you approach. You stop, stooping down to her level, and slowly reach out a hand to her. She rubs against your hand in a friendly gesture and enjoys your scratching behind her ears. You stay there some moments.

Your blood pressure lowers.

Your breathing slows down a bit, is steady and full.

Your mind disengages from the worries and concerns of just a few moments ago.

Your facial muscles relax.

Your eyes soften.

Your voice lowers to a soft tone.

You are speaking soothing word-sounds to the cat, a mantra to yourself as well as to her.

You feel the softness of her fur, the movement of her supple skin over her neck and shoulder bones.

The vibrations of her purring soothe you.

You are quiet. You are only here. Only now.

Then she's off to other places and adventures.

And you too continue on your way to other places and adventures, but changed by a gift from a cat.

> *Animals are such agreeable friends—they ask no questions, they pass no criticisms.*
>
> **—George Eliot**

Find an animal, make contact. Today.

Talking About Weather

How did it come to be that the phrase "talking about the weather" means talking about nothing important, or nothing in particular?

You only have to imagine the magnitude and variety and power of weather to see that Annie Dillard is surely right.

We always have weather to talk about, no matter what kind. It's also a safe subject; you can have strong opinions on what it's going to do, or whether or not you like what it's doing now, and no one will think the worse of you.

But the most potent aspect of the weather is that it is a colossal force over which we have no power. We live—and sometimes die—at its will.

Its effects on human life and history are evident and immense: It has caused the winning and losing of wars, the division and unity of nations, the discovery of continents, the crossing of mighty seas, the migrations of peoples, and the way our bodies are formed, and it is a significant control system of our entire universe—just for starters.

Those are good enough reasons, surely, to talk about it. But I think I know an even better one. The weather always affects how I feel; it always influences just how I am in this particular spot on the Earth. Always.

The power of weather over us is equal to the power of water over fish. And sometimes just as hard to notice. Talking about it helps us to become more aware of its power, and thus to become aware of our state of being just now, to know just how we are feeling—always good information to have.

There are seven or eight categories of phenomenon in the whole world worth talking about, and one of them is weather.

—Annie Dillard

Several times during the day, notice the weather, its changes, and how it is affecting you.

Holy Bridges

I think the meaning of this statement is that while other cultures in other times built cathedrals as the pinnacles of their cultural prowess, we build bridges. I'm not so sure this is true; we have some awesome cathedrals. But even so, our bridges are impressive as well, and the two have a few things in common.

A significant purpose of cathedrals was to provide, in the days before education was common, symbols and signs to teach faith and to remind people of those teachings. The hugeness of the building itself was the first and foremost symbol of what was most important in the community. Stained glass and graphic art were also important teaching aids.

But bridges can teach us too, if we see them with eyes open to symbols. They are the arteries that facilitate the movement of life within the community. Like cathedrals, they are conduits that facilitate bringing two distant places together. And, also like cathedrals, they show off what we can build. They are most often beautiful; by their nature, they seem daring and bold.

I easily bring to mind two important bridges in my life: one is huge and bold and industrial-looking; the other a one-lane, muddy path over some logs.

What bridges are in your life? What can you notice about them? A quiet mind sees that bridges can not only get us from here to there, but can be symbols to enrich the meaning of life.

Bridges are America's cathedrals.

—unknown

Learn today from your bridges: past, present, real, or symbolic.

Use Your Senses

Glory in all of the pleasures of the world. It's a message we don't often hear, or perhaps more accurately, we don't often hear it in a context of wholesomeness and integrity, and without guilt. Helen Keller, the American writer and lecturer, who was both blind and deaf from infancy, offers it to us in that context. "Make the most of every sense." Every day offers us feasts:

Look at shapes and colors. Trees. The sky at any time of day or night. The shape of a building. The color of a child's eyes. The picture on your wall. The reflection in your mirror. Your eyes, like an athlete's muscles, develop with training.

Listen to the world's sounds. A speeding train. Songs of birds. The tap-tap-tap of your computer's keys. Music. Your loved one's words, such as "Hi Mom, I'm home!" or "Hello Dear, how was your day?" or "I missed you so much!" To enhance what you hear, close your eyes for a moment.

Feel the world's textures. The feel of the cloth in your clothing. The handrail as you climb the stairs of a building. The erotic energy of your lover's touch. The skin is the body's largest organ. Spend a moment and notice what you feel on its entire surface at any given moment.

Taste the world's flavors. Chewing a macaroon. The taste of a postage stamp. Swallowing cold orange juice in the morning. Savoring tastes also has the advantage of slowing down your eating.

Smell the aroma of life. Passing by heliotrope or jasmine. Your perfume or aftershave. Someone else's. Walking into a very old house. A fragrance that reminds you of something long ago and far away. Especially when you want to remember something, pay attention to smell.

Make the most of every sense; glory in all of the pleasures and beauty which the world reveals to you. . . .

—Helen Keller

Make the most of every sense, today.

Observe Faces

I think I'll never tire of looking at faces, even of grumpy dictators, and whether deserved or not. (Can you deserve a face?) As I look, I muse:

Now there's a face that shows such care and compassion. And here is another, which shows suffering nobly borne.

His carries a deep anger and irritability—it's in the way he holds his mouth—which seems to indicate an unhappy man.

This child's face is all mirth! Such an unrestrained smile and uninhibited, delighted laughter.

There's a dour quality to that lady's face. I wonder what experiences have made her so? But no! Now that she smiles and laughs, how could I think her dour?

Shyness shines out of this man's eyes. I have a hunch he would make a good friend. His wife is by far the bolder; her eyes hold power.

Deep creases in sun-darkened skin, squinty and rheumy eyes, and wisps of white hair. He has been to the mountaintop and survived. I wonder if he is a good teacher? I'd bet so.

Reflect on the faces of your life. Perhaps take out some photos of family or friends, maybe of your grandparents. Contemplate those faces and notice what you see there.

And then stand quietly before a mirror, soften the muscles of your face, look with soft eyes, and smile.

At fifty everyone has the face he deserves.

—**George Orwell**

Today, notice the faces of people you encounter.

Snapshots

If you're like me, it almost goes without saying: Going on vacation? Take the camera. And how many pleasurable moments I enjoy looking over the snapshots from some past outing or adventure.

But taking a photograph does not mean that I will truly remember the moment, the place, and the persons the photograph captures. To truly remember, I must mindfully look, clearly see, and—most especially—deeply feel during the moments I am in their presence. Only then will I remember.

Mindfully look: This means to dwell some moments with the image before you, allowing the lines and colors and presence of the scene to make an impression on you.

Clearly see: Gaze, ponder, distinguish, compare. You might notice that the color of the marble in the building reminds you of the pink flesh of fresh salmon. The far sides of the mountains before you in the late afternoon sun actually are purple.

Deeply feel: The cityscape in your viewfinder brings back a memory of another time and place. The five people posed in a smiling and bantering group evokes a feeling of right now—this time, this place, these people, this light—that you want to keep.

These are what you first notice and remember, what will give depth, meaning, and insight to the way ahead. Then take the photo, which becomes the timeless vehicle of the moments it captures. Otherwise we have only snapshots, and the rest is lost, "returns to the changing winds."

Remember what you have seen, because everything forgotten returns to the changing winds.

—from a Navajo chant

Next outing: First look, and see, and notice your feeling. Then, take up your camera.

Realizing Life

At this point in Thornton Wilder's play, Emily is a ghost; she has just died and is allowed a brief visit back to life. The godlike stage manager gives, of course, the only real answer to her question: "No." But after a pause he adds, "The saints and poets, maybe—they do some."

I like this definition of saints and poets: they are everyone who has some capacity to realize life while they live it. That definition can include you and me, no matter who we are or how busy.

We don't have to be compared to Albert Schweitzer or have published books of poetry either. We just need, as much as we can, to realize life, now.

How do we realize life? Emily's ghost, who is allowed to return to Earth for her twelfth birthday, answers for us as she speaks to her mother who, still in human life, is—as mothers do and need to do—prattling on to her about eating slowly and keeping warm: "Oh, Mama, just look at me one moment as though you really saw me."

And then to the stage manager Emily says, "I can't. I can't go on. It goes so fast. We don't have time to look at one another. I didn't realize. So all that was going on and we never noticed."

Yes, it's all going on right now, today, this minute. Do you notice? Take Emily's advice: Look into the eyes of those you are with as though you were really seeing them, that is, attending to them as fully as you can, being aware as much as possible of all that is going on in the moment.

Do any human beings ever realize life while they live it?—every, every minute?

—**Emily in** *Our Town*

Join saints and poets. Today look at someone as though you were really seeing him or her.

Talking with Things

It is not unusual, in my practice as a family therapist, to hear someone very cautiously admit that they—only rarely, of course—talk to themselves, occasionally even out loud. Somehow, this practice has become associated with an expression of crazy behavior.

I believe it can often be a very healthy thing to do. It's a great way, for example, to cover all sides of an argument you're having with yourself. (The key, of course, is to know with whom you're talking.)

But what about not only talking to yourself but talking to things, and then having things talk to you? Have we gone over the edge here?

Can we really hear things talking to us? I would say yes and no. Take the no first: If I walk outside and ask the petunias for the time of day, please come and get me help. While the yes part of my answer is stronger, there is the qualification that Carver mentions: Things will talk to you only if you love them, and only if you have ears to hear.

What Carver, the brilliant agricultural scientist, teaches us with his words is what he must have experienced in his life. He worked with things like soybeans, sweet potatoes, and cotton and discovered hundreds of uses for them. He focused on them, he studied them, he learned all about them, he used them, tasted them, and lived with them.

He loved them. They spoke to him. They revealed to Carver the secrets they kept in their fleshy hearts.

He took time to listen to them. He was quiet enough to know he loved them, and they talked to him.

What part of this wondrous world do you love? Perhaps you already know that it talks to you. If not, listen carefully.

If you love it enough, anything will talk to you.

—George Washington Carver

Today notice what things you love. Then listen.

Overlooking

The other day when I was in a local bookstore, the owner recognized me from a recent book signing and, after greeting me, said, "I want to tell you how much I appreciate your story about your mother. I've used those words many times." My blank look encouraged her to continue: "How your mother said, 'I'm fine if you overlook a few things.'" Oh, yes, I recalled mentioning that, as a passing remark.

But she recognized a significance in the words that I had missed. Her recognition became mine when she gave it back to me.

Certainly one of the greatest challenges in our relationships—in raising children, thriving with a significant other, having friends, getting along with coworkers—is to know when to notice something and, especially, when not to notice. In other words, we have to learn a scale of priority with which we choose our issues; the lesser ones can slide, the greater ones we face.

My mother's words, spoken when she was aging quickly, are an example of how she picked her issues.

And now, how often the words come to me. How many opportunities I have to "overlook a few things": my own aches and pains, failings, frustrations, moments of impatience, or another person's fumbling, forgetfulness, or other foibles.

When we are stressed and overloaded, it's easy to lose a sense of proportion. But in the quiet times of life we can remember what is important and what is not so important, what to notice—and what not to notice.

"How are you today, Mom?"

"I'm fine—if you overlook a few things."

—from a conversation with my mother

Today be aware
of your choice:
To notice or
to overlook
a few things.

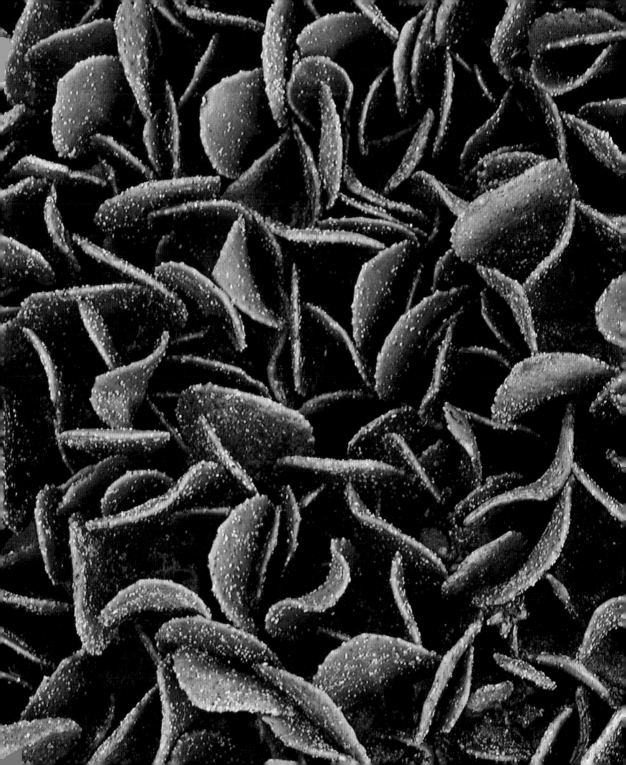

nine

Knowing Thyself

Invisibility

I was working with a client on stress management and asked him in my routine questioning if spirituality were part of his life. "No," he answered, "not at all. In fact I don't really know what you are talking about when you ask that."

I responded with a brief and uncareful definition of spirituality, thinking that this would give him a sense of what I meant.

"But that definition can mean anything and nothing," he said. "You really aren't telling me what it is. The word *spirituality* really makes no sense to me. It's just some well-intentioned but make-believe gibberish."

I engaged the challenge because, in many ways, his response was right on. My definition was intended for one who already accepted what I was talking about, not for someone who did not.

"What is valuable to you that is invisible, not directly perceivable by any of your senses?" I asked. In the process of answering he came to such values and meanings as "love of family" and "meaning of my faith" and "honesty" and "responsibility" and on and on. These are invisible in themselves, made visible only indirectly when they are acted out. They are beyond monetary value, ultimate, and essential. No one can be alive without them, although they certainly differ from person to person. We all have spirituality. It may or may not be part of a religious faith.

What is invisible is essential, says Saint-Exupéry, novelist, aviator, and adventurer. And what is invisible and essential becomes visible only to those with eyes to see, eyes that have been opened in quiet moments of stillness.

What is essential is invisible to the eye.

—**Antoine de Saint-Exupéry**

Take some moments today to name your invisible essentials.

Eulogy for a Wonderful Life

Bittersweet words these. How much better to realize how good life is—as much as possible—all along its course. That's one of the main purposes of achieving serenity, realizing life as you live it.

Colette, the French novelist who died at eighty-one in 1954, indeed had a full and meaningful life. She was a music-hall dancer, mime, socialite, wife—she married twice—and famous writer.

Most of us, especially when we compare ourselves to those we see as rich and famous, like Colette, feel that our lives are fairly dull and unimportant. Not so, if only we could realize it now.

So here's a suggestion to help the realization. Write your eulogy, what could be said about you at your funeral. It will feel, after the first moment perhaps, far from morbid; it will bring a new realization.

When I tried this process, the first thing I felt was panic. I couldn't think of anything to write, at least anything that I considered worth writing.

With persistence, it began to flow, not great and magnificent deeds—I still don't have those—but whom I loved, who loved me; what I valued and how I expressed it; when I was there for someone in need, and when I accepted their being there for me; what I really enjoyed and what made me laugh. Now I can go on and on. So can you.

This exercise has a bonus: as you prepare "what they can say about me when I'm gone" you will simultaneously create "what they can say about me while I'm here"! Your exercise will serve not only as a eulogy, but also as a reminder of the good things in your life right now.

What a wonderful life I've had! I only wish I'd realized it sooner.

—Colette

To realize your life, start writing your eulogy today.

The News

If you remember hearing those words on the radio, then you're, uh, . . . of a certain age. I recall hearing them as a boy listening to the evening news with my grandfather. Heatter, a popular news reporter of the day, would begin some newscasts with these words, trying to give hope during World War II, when most news was grim.

Most of the news is still grim. Or so it seems to me.

Perhaps more significant is that it's hard to get away from the news. At times, I try to take a vacation from watching the television news; it becomes a bit overwhelming to me. News dissemination is so constant and so widespread, however, that it is difficult not to get the news. And that has consequences.

We carry the news with us. We carry the crime, the violence, the wars, the suffering, and the pain. We carry more now than ever because we are bombarded by it constantly. This societal stress is relatively new to human life, and is added on to the already record-high personal stress that we each carry.

So we need to take charge, as much as possible, of how we allow the news into our lives:

A couple of times a week substitute Bach for Brokaw. You won't miss anything that you won't hear again soon.

Get in the habit of allowing a piece of news about suffering to trigger a moment of reflection for those involved. At least this is something we can do rather than just feeling powerless.

While you are watching the evening news, remember to breathe deeply, slowly.

Ah, there's good news tonight!

—**Gabriel Heatter**

Design your watching-the-news Stillpoint today.

Bird and Book

When I was a graduate student I learned one of the tenants of the field of psychotherapy: Don't accept gifts from clients. Accepting gifts is therapeutically ill-advised. It interferes with the process of therapy.

So when, during my early years as a family therapist at a social service agency, my client—I'll call him Ben—arrived for his session one day with a gift for me—a small, framed photograph of the coast—I told him that I could not accept it.

Now in my heart, and even in my clinically trained mind, I knew this gift was nothing more than Ben's way of saying thank you. It was the kind of thing he enjoyed doing. No hidden agendas. It would really be okay to accept this. But when he went on to say that he picked it specially for me while he and his wife were visiting the Wine Country north of San Francisco, I still said I was sorry but, no, I could not accept it. I also said something about rules for this sort of thing.

Ben left the session with his gift, and me uncomfortable with my decision to refuse it. To this moment, I regret my decision. I should have both accepted it and talked about it. But I followed the book I had read, not the bird I was looking at.

I'm not saying that the rule I learned is wrong, but that there are moments when you must trust what you see and feel right now, and not what the theory says, when you must trust the bird, not the book.

When the bird and the book disagree, always believe the bird.

—bird-watcher's proverb

Watch for opportunities today to trust the bird you see, not the book you've read.

Fads

What surprises me so much is not that I flit from one fad to another, from this hot idea to that one. No. What truly amazes me is the apparent ease with which I do it and how much company I have.

Last month I was focusing intently on the importance of a particular vitamin. This month someone asks me about it and I say, "Oh, yeah, I guess I ran out." Some intense importance!

A fad-dominated life is characterized by a distracted and vacant presence in the moment, by a never-ending string of disappointments, and by a palpable, but often inaccessible, sadness. It's like looking for fulfillment in way too many places. The new item that so excited me in anticipation now lies sadly forgotten—a betrayal—on the shelf.

In the young, this characteristic is probably a necessary stage of development. In adults, it is destructive because it keeps us from going deep—into our souls or into our projects—and limits maturity by keeping us stuck at a juvenile level. Of course, it is especially sad when we turn something momentous, like God, into a passing fad.

And let's not forget the formidable forces that drive the fads, and that benefit from them. Hot items sell. They have immediate interest. They entertain in the short run. They often fill an immediate urge. They are often difficult to resist.

Being still, for a while every day, and for a whole day every now and again, will clarify your fad-identifying vision.

> *In 1963 the mere mention of the God concept was good for a laugh. By 1965 it was many people's most serious concern.*
>
> **—Jeff Nuttall**

Identify a practice or project you want to stay with, go deeply into, or even return to.

Jump at the Sun

I appreciate this mother's effort to get her kids to become self-fulfilled. They are words of exuberance and hope. But jumping at the sun and barely getting off the ground are two different things.

Really, it's a wonderful statement of extremes: The goal is the sun, the flaming, all-consuming desire of pure ecstasy; the reality, a couple of inches off the Earth, for a couple of seconds.

I hope mothers still say things like that to their children. We need encouragement, especially when we are children, to become all that we can be.

I have the feeling, reading between the lines, that this mother was a woman who knew exactly what she was saying. If her words were taken literally, if you indeed were to land on the sun, you would long since have been incinerated to a mere speck of ash. But what a way to go!

Taken figuratively, the words seem to imply that the feeling of deepest passion and its achievement always involve suffering, an insight wise mothers know from lived experience. Thus her words both encourage—Jump for the highest goal you can think of!   and prepare for reality   Don't be surprised if you fall short, or if it's uncomfortably hot when you get there.

The saints and the poets know this. "Ah, but a man's reach should exceed his grasp, or what's a heaven for?" is Robert Browning's way to say it.

And many mothers and fathers know it too. "Jump at the sun!" is the way one of them said it.

Mama exhorted her children at every opportunity to "jump at the sun." We might not land on the sun, but at least we would get off the ground.

—Zora Neale Hurston

Who said,
"Jump at the sun!"
to you? To whom
can you say it?

116

Precious Bodies

No one would deny that we spend huge amounts of time, effort, and money trying to make our bodies more attractive.

I would make a suggestion for an additional effort: that we spend time seeing that the body we each have right now is already beautiful, awesome, and a wonder to behold.

But what about those twenty extra pounds, you might say, or my horrible hair, or my lack of hair, or the bags under my eyes? On and on we can go, focusing on all the things that make our bodies less than they should be.

When you take a moment to consider, you see those objections are based on a cultural projection. Many cultures, past and present, consider what we call too fat to be very appealing; what we call too thin to be provocative and attractive; what we call frumpy to be stylish. In present-day Western culture, only a narrowly defined type of human body is touted by the style-makers as attractive.

Somehow we ignore that only about one-fourth of one percent of people actually have that kind of body and they spend practically their whole lives keeping it that way so they can be photographed for the rest of us to feel bad about!

Crazy, right? But it takes time—quiet, reflective, contemplative time—to see the truth of this. The cultural forces telling you the opposite are strong. Today, be gentle and loving with your body.

Our body is precious. It is our vehicle for awakening. Treat it with care.

—**Jack Kornfield**

A suggestion to remember today: My body is beautiful just the way it is.

ten

Awakening to Wonder

Hello, Life

I'm convinced one of the reasons we enjoy it so much once we begin to spend time alone and quiet is that it encourages us to take life on its own terms and make the best of it. We become disinclined to say "No!" to the realities of life, and instead say, "Hello, where did you come from? We've not spent much time together, so sit down awhile and let's talk."

No matter how much I might desire and work for a totally balanced, peaceful, easygoing, work-free, and carefree life, I'm just not going to get it, at least most of the time. The more I cope with life on its terms, the more it will respond to my coping.

I can still picture the nurse who spoke the words above at a stress management seminar. These were not casually mouthed words, but spoken from the heart. She was suffering from burnout. She had an earnest look on her face, an expression of her deep concern that she would not be able to get going again if she were to give in to doing nothing.

Can you identify a fear that brings the same kind of worrisome words to your lips? Spend a moment with a little exercise. How would you finish this sentence?: "I'm afraid if I stop, I'll . . ."

By spending a long night of quiet reflection, this busy nurse was indeed able to start again, and to keep on starting again, because during that quiet time she learned to engage her challenges ("Hello, life") rather than avoid them ("No!").

I'm afraid if I stop, I'll never be able to start again.

—nursing seminar participant

Begin a dialogue with the challenging aspects of your life today.

Covering Up

No, you can't get away from yourself, but you can cover yourself, you can avoid whatever you don't want to face, by going to a booze-bazaar. The language of this saying from the 1920s is quaint to our ears, but its truth remains real.

And how good we are at covering! Often we don't even know we're doing it. We get into deep trouble by covering because what we cover is almost always what we need to face and resolve. Consider just a few covers:

Alcohol and drugs are perhaps the most common ones. A few drinks or pills, and the pain of loss or the agony of fear is less demanding, easier to ignore or forget.

Television covers a lot. Turn it on when you get home, turn it off when you go to bed. It's always filling in time that might otherwise bring you to...what?

Humor is also a way to cover. It's often difficult to name it because the response is that you just can't take a joke. If you know someone who always jokes about the issue, you've probably discovered a cover.

Work is certainly one of the most common ways to cover what we don't want to face. It has the "advantages" of being socially acceptable and often profitable. Covers are endless: food, religion, hobbies, self-righteousness; literally anything can be a cover.

For those who would like to be awake, dis-covering our covering is not only essential but enormously rewarding: You get yourself back.

You can't get away from yourself by going to a booze-bazaar.

—Elbert Hubbard

Take quiet time today to discover your ways—maybe just little ones— of covering.

Failing

Recently I received a phone call—a recorded message actually—that told me that my services were no longer needed at the place where I had a part-time job. I enjoyed the work I did there and looked forward to it. Now, quite suddenly, I had been dropped.

The administrator who called was clear and kind; I could tell he was sorry, and he said so in a gentle way. The reasons he gave were understandable; I would have come to the same conclusion, given the circumstances.

But the thought that came to me immediately—not thought really, but feeling—was, I have failed. What did I do wrong? I've been terminated, sent packing, dismissed. I've failed!

Well, yes. . . . But have I failed, really? There's a fine line here. On the one hand, the fact is they let me go. So in a sense, yes, I have failed. I would feel somehow dishonest, not allowed my truth, no matter how unwelcome, if someone tried to tell me that I didn't in some way fail. On the other hand, trying something, failing, then trying again, is the way to most good and great deeds. Trying again—that's the key.

"America's Sweetheart," Mary Pickford, the plucky film star of the 20s, tells it clearly: Failure is not falling down but *staying* down.

Thus I guess the question for me is clear: That's over, how can I try again?

> This thing we call "failure" is not the falling down, but the staying down.
>
> —Mary Pickford

Think of something you consider a failure. Can you—or did you—get up and go on? The only failure is staying down.

121

Telling the World

The most effective step in dealing with any fear is to some way, any way, tell it to the world. If you don't do this, the fear will get stuck. It must be told!

This process can be exquisitely simple: Have you ever had the experience of feeling better, feeling relieved, because you had just gotten something off your chest and told a friend about it?

The process can be magnificent and it doesn't have to be only in words. Listen to Beethoven's *Ninth Symphony*, for example, and you are experiencing that composer's narration of his strong, brooding fears, his deep hope for joy. He narrates them in music. Or you can dance your fear, or sculpt it, or draw it, or write it, and so on. Literally anything can serve as a telling to the world.

The narration can also be entertaining. When I first read the above quote from Alfred Hitchcock, I was struck with his clear, simple statement of narrating. What he feared, he expressed to the world in scary, suspenseful films. As we experience his fears through the film (I think of the way I felt watching *Dial M for Murder* and *Rear Window*), they become less of a burden for him. By his process of narration, we participate in his fears.

But we not only share these fears; they also serve us. Artists, like the musical composer and film director, have expressed to us, have entrusted us with, their feelings. The resultant music and films are wonderfully beneficial: The symphony lifts our spirits, the film delights and entertains us. Narrating puts you in touch with the world and the world in touch with you.

The only way to get rid of my fears is to make films about them.

—Alfred Hitchcock

Try to find a way to express something you fear to some part—big or small—of the world today.

Reframing Grief

Often what prevents us from creating quiet space in our lives, what keeps us from the essential joy of doing nothing, is the presence of grief. It is a formidable presence and, understandably, our first response is to avoid it.

Grief is always about loss, the anguish and pain we feel when we lose someone or something precious to us. And it regularly happens to all of us. It is one of our most familiar common grounds. No one is immune.

I believe one of the first signs that we are ready to face grief is our willingness to stop, to be quiet, and to be with ourselves.

This is a sign of the sacredness that author Molly Fumia speaks about. Grief is sacred because it can, perhaps more than anything, bring us into contact with ourselves. (In her brilliant and powerful book *Honor Thy Children*, Fumia relates the story of parents' loss of all three of their children, and of their journey to a noble response.)

So consider: What am I sad about today? Then just allow the feeling of loss, the grief, to be there a moment.

Even though grief involves fear and pain, and even though we initially run from such things, Fumia continues, the "sacredness is in the sound of our returning footsteps." Having grieved, we return to life, to ourselves, with a new compassion, a new understanding, and even a new joy.

In grief we face a sacred moment, one permeated with fear, overflowing with pain, steeped in difficulty.

—Molly Fumia

Today spend some time feeling one of your losses, and listen for the sound of (or the promise of) your returning footsteps.

Where Am I?

Where are you and where are you going? If we know the answers to these questions, Lincoln reminds us in his direct, unadorned style, we can make much better life decisions.

I would add: We must not only attempt to know the answers, but we make every effort to remember them, and keep them up-to-date.

Some years ago, I was at a seminar presented by the well-known author Sam Keen. He gave a wonderful example of Lincoln's truth. He was speaking of marriage, and, if memory serves, of his own experience.

Too many of us, he taught, make the decision to choose a life partner before we begin to answer Lincoln's questions for ourselves. The result is that, because we are not clear about where we are, nor about where we want to go, we are in poor position to pick a lifelong companion for the journey; if we get the right one, it's more a matter of luck than wisdom.

One of the best times for a long period of doing nothing, a Grinding Halt, is before a major decision, like choosing a life partner, having a child, changing your work, reentering the work world, retiring from work, or moving across the country.

It's during a long time of peace and quiet that you have a chance to begin the process of forming answers to Lincoln's questions.

If we could first know where we are and whither we are tending, we could better judge what to do and how to do it.

—Abraham Lincoln

Are there major decisions ahead for you? Schedule a Grinding Halt now.

Just Being

In a *New Yorker* cartoon, Gahan Wilson shows two Buddhist monks seated next to each other, quiet, still, meditating. One is very old and experienced in the ways of meditation. The other is young and has a perplexed look on his face. It's evident that he has just asked his more experienced mentor a question. The old monk's answer to the question is: "Nothing happens next. This is it."

I like the cartoon because I have often identified with the young monk. "What happens next? Isn't the idea that something is supposed to happen? When nothing happens, isn't that a waste of time?"

I also like it because it has a clear and important message for the way we live in these millennial times. Like the young monk, we need the wisdom of people who have spent time being quiet, listening to the heart, learning the questions that only silence can reveal, absorbing the life-giving silence, and being as aware as possible of this moment.

We need old wisdom. The wisdom of crones and shamans, of wise priests and rabbis, of discerning souls who have spent time on the mountaintop.

The young monk's question is based on a firmly established assumption in our Western minds: It's what *happens* that's important. And, of course, often that's true. But what happens is also the part that is easy for us to understand. The part we don't understand is the old monk's answer, "Nothing *happens* next." There is no event, but there is something. There is, in fact, everything.

The cartoon implies that when the old monk is long gone, the young monk will be there to take his place and thus the wisdom will continue.

Nothing happens next. This is it.

—Gahan Wilson

Today, as you move through your day, remember that this is it.

The Inner Connection

There is a most wonderful quality that results from the time we spend alone and recollected. The comfort we feel with our own inner selves will be recognized by others who are also accustomed to going within, and we won't miss the subtle invitations to intimacy and connectedness.

I remember a moment when this inner connection with another person happened for me. I was going through a significant life transition and I had just spent a long period of time alone, a month-long Grinding Halt. Soon after, I attended a large family gathering where I met for the first time the wife of one of my cousins. The moment our eyes met, I knew that she was someone with an awareness of her inner life, and an open welcome to others who would connect with her, including me.

But I felt very vulnerable and I was not ready to take the risk of opening myself up to her. So I ran, quite literally I'm a bit embarrassed to say, to the other end of the room and started a much safer conversation. I knew, from the inner connection, that she would know everything about me in about three minutes of conversation, and I wasn't ready.

Something in her and something in me connected—the inner connection—and communicated without words.

In the meantime, happily, I have been able to tell the story to the same woman, now a friend as well as a cousin.

The more time you spend in quiet recollection, the more you will notice others who do the same, and the more you will take the risk to connect with them.

Intimacy requires courage because risk is inescapable. We cannot know at the outset how the relationship will affect us.

—**Rollo May**

> Be open today to recognize an inner connection with others who also spend time with the genuine within.